500

cake & cupcake decorations

500

cake & cupcake decorations

the only cake & cupcake decorating compendium you'll ever need

Amanda Rawlins & Caroline Deasy

SELLERS
PUBLISHING

A Quintet Book

Published by Sellers Publishing, Inc.
161 John Roberts Road, South Portland, Maine 04106
Visit our Web site: www.sellerspublishing.com
E-mail: rsp@rsvp.com

ISBN: 978-1-4162-0910-2
e-ISBN: 978-1-4162-0963-8
Library of Congress Control Number: 2013931213
QTT.FHCB

This book was conceived, designed, and produced by
Quintet Publishing Limited
6 Blundell Street
London N7 9BH
United Kingdom

Photographer: Tim Bowden
Food Stylists: Amanda Rawlins & Caroline Deasy
Designer: Jacqui Caulton
Art Director: Michael Charles
Series Editor: Donna Gregory
Publisher: Mark Searle

10 9 8 7 6 5 4 3 2 1

Printed in China by 1010 Printing International Ltd.

contents

introduction

Cake decorating is loads of fun and this comprehensive volume features a bounty of accessible recipes and clear step-by-step instructions that guarantee success every time. The book also includes valuable information about the materials and equipment you'll need to get the best results. Authors (and sisters!) Amanda Rawlins and Caroline Deasy present expert advice on baking, basic recipes for cakes and frosting, buttercream piping techniques, a how-to section on cake stacking, and a multitude of helpful tips.

- the book's organization provides easy access to recipes and techniques with clear directions
- six chapters show how to decorate cakes and cupcakes for celebrations and occasions, and to create embellishments, flowers, letters and numbers, and animals
- includes overviews of decorating with sugar paste, fondant, gum paste, and flower paste, plus a section on other useful techniques.

This truly is the only cake & cupcake decorating compendium you'll ever need!

tools & equipment

baking equipment

cookie scoops: either 3 tablespoons
    for cupcakes or 1 1/2 teaspoons for
    mini cupcakes
round or square baking pans for your cake size
12-cupcake muffin pan or 24-mini-cupcake
    muffin pan
measuring spoons

cooling rack
liners (regular and mini)
parchment paper
cake boards or drums to match the size
    of your cake
stand mixer or handheld mixer

decorating tools

Here is a selection of the decorating tools used in this book. They are widely available at craft stores and sugarcraft specialty shops. Although they are recommended, most are not essential and you can find a multitude of alternatives in your kitchen; piping tips are perfect for small circle cutters and kitchen knives for a blade tool. For almost all of the projects in this book, you will need at least a rolling pin, a craft knife, edible glue, clean paintbrush, toothpicks and wooden skewers; these have therefore not been listed in the individual equipment lists for each project.

piping bags
piping tips
cutters in various shapes
spatula

modeling tools
toothpicks and wooden skewers
sugar-paste smoother
craft knife

retailers

Many craft stores and large grocery stores stock a good range of cake decorating equipment and materials. You can also purchase online from many suppliers, including the following:

www.michaels.com
www.wilton.com
www.globalsugarart.com

www.sweetwise.com
www.icingonlinestore.com
www.joann.com

baking & cake preparation tips

- Once you have chosen the cake decoration project you wish to make, read the instructions all the way through. Many of decorations require time to set or dry, so factor this into your timeframe.

- Decide how many servings you wish to make: A 6-inch cake will yield 6-8 portions; an 8-inch cake will yield 12–15 portions; a 10-inch cake will yield 25–30 portions.

- All cake projects in this book give the appropriate-sized cake to start with, but they can all be modified to suit smaller or larger cakes.

- If you are not a confident baker, there is no shame in using a store-bought cake mix. An 18.25-oz. box will yield an 8-inch cake (or 18 cupcakes).

- Remember to always let cakes cool completely before beginning to decorate. Buttercream and sugar paste will both melt if the cake is even a little warm.

- Always work in a cool room when using buttercream and sugar paste.

- Wrap cooled, undecorated sponge cakes in plastic wrap and keep in a cool, dry place for 2–3 days. Cakes decorated with sugar paste can be placed in a cake box (not an airtight container) in a cool, dry, dark place for up to a week.

- Buttercream-frosted cupcakes can be kept in the refrigerator for 4–5 days. Any sugar paste decorations for buttercream-frosted cupcakes should be placed at the last minute.

vanilla sponge cake

Superfine sugar gives a lovely light-textured cake, but if you can't find it, plain granulated sugar is a good substitute. The glycerin is optional, but will keep the cake moist for longer; if you are making the cake a few days ahead of serving, it is a good idea.

for a 6-inch cake:
1 1/2 sticks (6 oz.) unsalted butter, room temperature
3/4 cup (6 oz.) superfine sugar
1/2 tsp. glycerin (optional)
3 medium eggs
1 1/2 cups (6 oz.) self-rising flour
1/2 tsp. vanilla extract

for an 8-inch cake:
2 1/2 sticks (10 oz.) unsalted butter, room temperature
1 1/4 cups (10 oz.) superfine sugar
1 tsp. glycerin (optional)
5 medium eggs
2 1/2 cups (10 oz.) self-rising flour
1 tsp. vanilla extract

for a 10-inch cake:
4 sticks (16 oz.) unsalted butter, room temperature
2 cups (16 oz.) superfine sugar
1 1/2 tsp. glycerin (optional)
8 medium eggs
4 cups (16 oz.) self-rising flour
2 tsp. vanilla extract

Preheat the oven to 350°F (180°C). Line two round cake pans of the relevant size with parchment paper.

In a large bowl, cream the butter, sugar, and glycerin (if using) until pale and fluffy. Beat in the eggs, one at a time, with a tablespoon of the flour and add in the vanilla extract. Mix until the ingredients are combined. Add the remaining flour and continue to beat until light and fluffy.

Divide between the two pans and bake for: 25–30 minutes for a 6-inch cake; 35–40 minutes for an 8-inch cake; and 50–55 minutes for a 10-inch cake. You may need to loosely cover the top of the cake with foil, or turn the oven down to 325°F (160°F) if the cakes brown too much before a skewer inserted into the middle comes out clean. Leave to stand in the pans for 10 minutes before turning out onto cooling racks.

rich chocolate cake

for a 6-inch cake:
2/3 cup (2 oz) cocoa powder
3/4 cup + 1tbsp. boiling water
1 stick (4 oz.) unsalted butter,
    softened
1 cup + 2 tbsp. (8 oz.)
    superfine sugar
2 medium eggs
1 cup + 2 tbsp. (5 oz.) all-
    purpose flour
3/8 tsp. baking soda
1/4 tsp. baking powder

for an 8-inch cake:
1 cup (3 1/4 oz.) cocoa
    powder
1 1/2 cups boiling water
1 2/3 sticks (6 3/4 oz.)
    unsalted butter, softened
2 cups (14 oz.) superfine
    sugar
3 large eggs
2 cups (9 oz.) all-purpose
    flour
3/4 tsp. baking soda
1/2 tsp. baking powder

for a 10-inch cake:
1 2/3 cups (5 oz.) cocoa
    powder
2 1/3 cups boiling water
2 2/3 sticks (10 1/2 oz.)
    unsalted butter, softened
3 cups + 1 tbsp. (1 lb 6 oz)
    superfine sugar
5 large eggs
3 cups + 2 tbsp. (14 oz.)
    all-purpose flour
1 1/4 tsp. baking soda
3/4 tsp. baking powder

Preheat the oven to 350°F (180°C). Mix the cocoa powder with the boiling water and allow to cool. Line two round cake pans of the relevant size with parchment paper. Cream the butter and sugar and until pale and fluffy. Beat in the eggs, 1 at a time, with a tablespoon of the flour to avoid curdling. Mix until the ingredients are combined. Add the remaining flour, and the baking soda and powder alternately with the cocoa–water mixture and fold into the remaining mixture until combined.

Divide between the two pans and bake for: 25–30 minutes for a 6-inch cake; 35–40 minutes for an 8-inch cake; and 50–55 minutes for a 10-inch cake. You may need to loosely cover the top of the cake with foil, or turn the oven down to 325°F (160°F) if the cakes brown too much before a skewer inserted into the middle comes out clean. Leave to stand in the pans for 10 minutes before turning out onto cooling racks.

cupcakes

Use half of the 8-inch quantities of either of the recipes on pages 12 and 15 to make 12 cupcakes. Line the muffin pan with 12 cupcake liners. Use a tablespoon to evenly distribute the batter among the liners. The batter should fill half to two thirds of the liner. Or, to ensure even-size cupcakes, use a 3-tablespoon cookie scoop. Bake at the same temperature for 17–20 minutes. For a whip frosting, pipe 3 tablespoons buttercream per cupcake; for a flat frosting, use 1 tablespoon buttercream per cake.

mini cupcakes

Use half of the 8-inch quantites of either of the recipes on pages 12 and 15 to make 24 mini cupcakes and use a 1 1/2-teaspoon cookie scoop to ensure even cupcakes. Bake at the same temperature for 12–14 minutes. For a whip frosting, pipe 1 tablespoon buttercream per cupcake; for a flat frosting, use 1 1/2 teaspoons buttercream per cake.

cake pops

To make 8 cake pops, use half of the 8-inch quantites of either of the recipes on pages 12 and 15 and bake in a 9-inch square pan for 25 minutes. Once cool, crumble the cake and mix the crumbs with 2–3 tablespoons buttercream, a little bit at a time until cake is moist and can hold a ball shape, yet still slightly crumbly. Use your hands to incorporate the frosting into the cake crumbs. Use a mini ice cream scoop and scoop out two balls of cake mixture. Roll the mixture into a tight ball and place on a plate. Repeat until all the cake mixture has been rolled into balls. Insert a cake pop stick into each ball, and freeze for 20 minutes. Remove from the freezer, dip each in melted chocolate to cover with a thin coating, and stand in a styrofoam stand to dry. Store in a cool place.

buttercream

To fill a 6-in. cake: 1/2 stick (2 oz.) butter and 1 cup (4 oz.) confectioners' sugar
To top, fill, and side-coat a 6-in. cake: 2 sticks (8 oz.) butter and 4 cups (1 lb.) confectioners' sugar
To fill an 8-in. cake: 1 stick (4 oz.) butter and 2 cups (8 oz.) confectioners' sugar
To top, fill, and side-coat an 8-inch cake: 3 sticks (12 oz.) butter and 6 cups (1 1/2 lb.) confectioners' sugar
To frost 12 cupcakes or 24 mini cupcakes: 2 sticks (8 oz.) butter and 4 cups (1 lb.) confectioners' sugar

Beat the confectioners' sugar and butter together until smooth. Add vanilla extract or unsweetened cocoa powder for flavoring, if desired. You can simply cover the cake or cupcakes with the buttercream using a palette knife, or use piping effects (see buttercream piping techniques, page 25). If you live in a high humidity environment, add 1 to 2 tsp. of meringue powder to buttercream make it more resistant to moisture in the air.

royal icing

5 1/2 cups (1 lb 7 oz.) confectioner's sugar, sifted
2 tbsp dried egg white
6 tbsp water

Mix all the ingredients together with an electric mixer on a low speed for 8-10 minutes or until the icing loses its shine. Add more water a teaspoon at a time if it appears too stiff. It needs to be the right consistency to pipe. One of the most important things to get right in decorating cakes is the consistency of the royal icing. Drag a knife through the surface of the icing and count to 25. If the icing surface becomes smooth in anywhere between 20–25 seconds, the icing is ready to use for detailing work. Cover with damp paper towels to stop the icing drying out.

preparing cake for sugar-paste covering

Even top of the cake by slicing any dome tops off of both cakes. Sandwich the cakes together with buttercream and seedless jelly, ensuring the bottom of the cake layer faces up. You may need to trim the edges to remove any crust, which may show through the sugar paste.

Place cake on a cake board or drum 1 inch bigger than the cake. Crumb-coat the cake, providing glue to the sugar paste by covering the whole cake with a thin layer of buttercream. You can also place a table knife in a glass of freshly boiled water and skim the cake to provide an even surface. Refrigerate the cake, preferably overnight, to firm the cake and buttercream.

covering cake with sugar paste

When you are ready to cover the cake with sugar paste, remove the cake from the refrigerator.

Lightly cover a flat surface with cornstarch and roll out the desired color sugar paste in a circle to 1/4-inch thickness. Lift the sugar paste over the cake to cover and use your hands to gently smooth the sugar paste over the cake.

If you get any air bubbles, pop with a pin and gently smooth out with your finger. Using a cake smoother, start at the top and smooth the sugar paste to ensure a flat and even surface. Repeat on the side of the cake. Trim the excess sugar paste with a knife.

Covering a cake in sugar paste keeps the sponge moist for up to a week after baking. This allows you to bake ahead and finish the cake decoration prior to a big event or occasion.

how much sugar paste?

Most colored sugar paste comes in packages of 4 or 8 oz, and white sugar paste most often comes in 8, 16, or 24 oz packages. To make the individual projects in this book, the quantities will depend on the number and size of the cakes, cupcakes, or cake pops you wish to make. If you are decorating either one cake or 12 cupcakes, you will normally need only one 8 oz package of each color listed. If you are planning on making more than this, you will need more. Often, you won't use the whole package; wrap any leftovers tightly in plastic wrap and store in a cool, dark place for up to a month.

If you're decorating a cake and covering it with sugar paste or rolled fondant, use this handy guide to help you cover your cake successfully:

heart & round		square	
diameter	sugar paste needed	width/height	sugar paste needed
6–7 inches	1 lb 2 oz	6 inches	1 lb 2 oz
8 inches	1 lb 10 oz	7 inches	1 lb 10 oz
9 inches	2 lb 3 oz	8 inches	2 lb 3 oz
10 inches	2 lb 12 oz	9 inches	2 lb 12 oz
11 inches	3 lb 5 oz	10 inches	3 lb 5 oz
12 inches	3 lb 14 oz	11 inches	3 1b 14 oz
		12 inches	4 lb 6 oz

multilayer cake stacking

Stacking cakes involves the use of 4 cake dowels (available from specialty shops) or long straws and cake boards, which are often made from strong corrugated cardboard, trimmed to the shape of your cake, and wrapped with foil or decorative wraps.

Once the cakes have been covered with sugar paste, allow to dry for 24 hours before stacking.

Place the base cake on a cake board or drum. Insert the 4 dowels into the base cake the complete height of the layer, within the diameter of the cake above. Mark the height of the dowels with a pencil, remove, and cut the dowels. Reinsert the dowels and then you can place the next cake on top, with the cake board between.

Repeat the process for additional layers. If you are using a mix of fruitcake and sponge cake, make sure that the fruitcake is on the lower layer, as it is heavier and will ensure stability. If you are planning to transport the multilayer cake, it will be safer to assemble in situ.

buttercream piping techniques

In addition to a simple covering of buttercream, you can also add some cool piping techniques to decorate your cake and cupcakes.

tips for using a piping bag

You can use a piping bag, fitted with a small tip, to pipe buttercream onto cupcakes or cakes.

- To assemble a piping bag, simply insert the metal or plastic tip through the large opening in the bag until the tip has come through the smaller opening in the piping bag.

- To fill the bag, hold the bag with one hand and spoon the piping mixture in with the other.

- It's much easier to place a piping bag in a drinking glass to fill it with buttercream...no mess!

- To pipe, you need both hands. Holding the bag so it is horizontal, put your fingertip over the end of the tip; then, with the other hand, twist and squeeze the large end of the bag until you can feel that you've moved the piping mixture all the way to the tip and the bag is firm.

- Practice piping on a piece of baking paper before attempting to decorate cupcakes or cakes. Aim the bag with one hand and squeeze with the other to pipe. When the detail is completed, hold the tip down, then bring it up sharply to stop piping.

- Add sprinkles, sugar pearls or candies while the icing is still wet.

coloring buttercream

Buttercream is cream in color, so consider this when adding color. Using the whitest butter/ unsalted butter will produce a whiter buttercream.

Liquid food coloring is ideal for pastel shades, but will not produce intense color. For this, you need to use color pastes. However, there is a warning! To obtain vibrant colors like red, black, and purple, you will need to use a lot of coloring to achieve the color you require, resulting in a runnier and bitter-tasting buttercream. The other side effect you may find is that your guests are walking around with purple or black mouths after eating. There are "extra-color" pastes on the market, which require less paste to produce a vibrant result (e.g., red extra color paste).

multicolor buttercream

This technique allows you to mix more than one frosting color and create some cool effects. Place your piping bag with desired tip in a drinking glass and fill each side with a different color frosting. Squeeze the piping bag and practice a few strokes.

fire = red, yellow, and orange
water = white and blue

covering cakes using piping effects

You can use a number of piping techniques to cover your cakes. This includes ruffles using a Wilton no. 104 tip, which you pipe vertically around the side of the cake. Use a Wilton no. 1 tip to pipe swirl roses all over the cake, or a Wilton no. 12 tip to create the pipe-and-push petal effect.

frosting a cupcake with a whip

Fill a piping bag with desired colored frosting and use a Wilton 1M tip to swirl the top of the cupcake. Start at the back of the cupcake, swirl around the edge, and then continue inward to fill; release pressure and pull away. Now pipe a smaller second ring in the center to form a peak. Add decorations before the frosting sets.

grass or hair

Color the frosting green and use a Wilton no. 233 tip (multi-opening). Practice a few strokes by applying pressure to cake and then pulling away to create grass. The same method can be used to give the effect of hair.

hand-piped roses

Fill the piping bag with the desired color frosting and use a Wilton no. 104 rose tip. You can either pipe onto a small piece of parchment paper on a piping nail and then transfer to the cake or cupcake after piping, or pipe directly onto a cupcake.

sugar paste, fondant, gum paste & flower paste

Sugar paste is the professional term for fondant. Gum paste and Mexican modeling paste (MMP) can be used as alternatives to fondant for modeling, as it dries harder. Although edible, it's not palatable. It's ideal for cake toppers, but we wouldn't recommend its use in cupcake decorations. Flower paste is essentially sugar paste with additional ingredients to allow it to be rolled very thin, and it dries very hard. It's more expensive than sugar paste or fondant, and it's essential for making very delicate flowers (like the moth orchid on page 186), but not essential for basic flowers like daisies and small rosebuds.

making cake & cupcake decorations from sugar paste

Sugar paste is pliable and then turns hard enough to support itself when dry. To make the sugar paste pliable, knead it on a surface dusted with cornstarch. You can then mold it or roll it out to cut out decorations freehand or with cutters.

Once you have made your decoration, we would suggest laying it on parchment paper on a flat surface. Most decorations call for a 24-hour drying time, but many will probably support their own weight after a few hours. Once dry, your decorations will keep for at least two weeks, which is ideal when you are creating a celebration cake and cupcakes and want to get ahead, instead of creating a masterpiece that morning!

coloring sugar paste

Even though there is a wide range of colored sugar pastes on the market, you can easily color white sugar paste to your desired color by using food color pastes. For pastel shades, use a toothpick to dot the desired color food coloring into the sugar paste. Knead onto a surface dusted with confectioners' sugar until you reach the desired shade. You may need to add another dot of food coloring.

Alternatively, if you have primary-color sugar paste, you can mix a small amount of the desired color to white sugar paste to reach your desired shade. It's just like mixing paint colors:

pink = white + red
lemon = white + yellow
lilac = white + grape
tan = white + brown or chocolate flavored sugar paste
skin tones = white + light or dark brown sugar paste

color effects
The versatility of sugar paste allows you to mix a number of colors to create some cool effects:

water = white + pale blue + blue
marble = white + small amount of black
wood = brown + small amount of tan
parchment = tan + small amount of brown

Roll the colors into equal length sausages and then roll together, fold in half, and press together. Repeat the process until you reach the desired effect. The key is not to overmix the sugar paste to blend the colors. Roll out the sugar paste and use as directed.

modeling

Remember Play-Doh when you were a child? Sugar paste is exactly the same! You can create almost anything out of sugar paste.

cutters

There is a vast array of cutters available in both supermarkets and specialty stores, and you will probably already have a few in your kitchen drawers. You can also be imaginative with what you have in your kitchen; piping tips are perfect for small circles and drinking glasses for larger circles.

templates

If the recipe calls for a cutter you do not have, you can easily draw the shape on paper, cut it out, and place the template on the rolled sugar paste; cut out with a craft knife. You can tidy the edges of your cutout with either the edge of the knife or your finger.

frilling

Frilling is good for skirts, blankets, and other fabrics. We have also used it in our rosette. This effect can be achieved by placing a skewer over the edge of the sugar paste where the taper of the skewer starts, and gently rolling.

patterned sugar paste

You can create fun patterns on the sugar paste by scattering small pieces of contrasting-color sugar paste and rolling them in to create camouflage and animal prints.

embossing mats & texture rolling pins

There is a whole range of embossing mats and texture rolling pins to use on rolled sugar paste to create a 3-D raised or imprinted pattern, including damask, flowers, and swirls. To prevent sticking, paint a small amount of vegetable oil onto the mat before embossing, and remove excess with a paper towel.

stamps

You can use a range of raised craft stamps to imprint the sugar paste with details, including letters. Ideal for names and messages.

silicone molds

These have become increasingly popular to create 3-D shapes. Simply paint the inside of the mold with a small amount of vegetable oil to prevent sticking, press in the sugar paste, and remove. You can also buy silicone kits to create your own molds to suit your cake design.

stencils

Sheet stencils are widely available to transfer a design onto sugar paste, either rolled or directly onto a cake using edible luster dust or luster sprays.

letter & number tappits

You can use alphabet cutters or sugarcraft tappits for letters and numbers. These are press cutters that you "tap" out of. To ease in the release of the letters or numbers, roll out the sugar paste to 2 mm thick and allow to dry for 5 minutes before using.

other decorating techniques

hand-painting
Edible paints are widely available and you can apply to dried sugar paste just like a canvas.
If you would like more of an oil paint effect, you can add a small amount of melted cocoa
butter. Alternatively, you can add clear alcohol to edible luster dust to create paint.

brush embroidery
Create a stunning lace effect by piping the outline of flowers or lace using royal icing and a
no. 2 tip. Using a flat-headed brush, stroke the icing inward and add details.

hand-piping royal icing
You can make royal icing yourself (see recipe page 19) or buy it ready-made. Use a no. 2 tip
to pipe dots or swags directly onto cakes and cupcakes.

sugar & icing sheets
These sheets of patterned or printed icing can be cut with scissors or used with cutters and
adds a different design to decorations.

marzipan or almond paste
Can be used as an alternative to sugar paste and is commonly used in molding fruits and
vegetables. Can be a tastier option for larger edible decorations.

edible pens
You can easily draw or write on hardened sugar paste.

luster spray

Creates a pearlized, gold, or silver finish when sprayed on hardened sugar paste.

edible glitter

Edible glitter in various colors adds a sparkle to decorations or frosting.

candies, nonpareils & sprinkles

Ideal for small details like eyes and noses. Candies can also be rolled out to achieve a new medium.

other edibles

Try cookie crumbs, marshmallows, or edible flowers. You can use cookies to provide sand and dirt effects; chocolate sticks and wafer rolls can give structural strength when required.

non-edible alternatives

Try feathers, diamante toppers, or paper picks. Use custom printing and laminated toppers for a personalized effect. It's easy to craft personalized cupcake toppers using a computer and color printer, and then laminating the results. Laminating ensures that they are food safe, but you should make your guests aware that these toppers are not edible. You can personalize them with names, ages, favorite characters, and even photos...their use is endless. You can also enhance your cakes with store-bought cake toppers. Diamante initials and brooches provide a classy effect, as do feathers and sprays.

celebration

Every celebration merits a party, and every party

needs a cake! Here are plenty of beautiful ideas to

help you celebrate in style.

new-baby teddy bear mini cupcakes

see variations page 60

Welcome new arrivals with these sweet little cupcake toppers.

mini cupcakes baked in tan liners (page 16)
1 1/2 tbsp. chocolate buttercream per cupcake
  (page 19)
sugar paste in white, light brown, and dark
  brown

equipment
mini teddy bear cutter or template
black edible pen

Roll out the light brown sugar paste to 1/10 in. thick. Using the mini teddy bear cutter, cut out the teddy bear shapes from the sugar paste. Blend a small amount of light brown with white sugar paste to create a pale brown color. Roll a small ball 1/4 in. wide and press with your finger to create the snout. Add the snout to the face and indent a smile and lips with a craft knife.

Add a small dark brown sugar-paste nose to the face. Using a toothpick, prick the seams of the teddy bear at the arms and legs to create a stitching effect. Roll two tiny white sugar-paste balls to create the buttons and secure to the chest. Prick two holes in each button. Use a black edible pen to mark the eyes.

Repeat the process for each cupcake. You can create coordinating bears by alternating the color tones of pale brown, light brown, and dark brown. Allow to dry and add to the tops of the frosted mini cupcakes.

christening cross cake

see variations page 61

This simple motif is perfectly suited to christenings, but you can use the flowers to fill in any shape you like.

8-in. square sponge cake covered with white
   sugar paste (pages 12, 20)
sugar paste in red and white

equipment
1/2-in-wide blossom flower plunger cutter
sponge mat

Mix a small amount of red into the white sugar paste to create a medium pink. Roll out the medium pink sugar paste to 1/10 in. thick and use the flower plunger cutter to cut blossoms. Push and release the blossom straight onto the sponge mat with a little pressure, as this will give it a raised, 3-D effect. Repeat the process to make about 100 medium pink blossoms.

Allow to dry for at least 10 minutes on the sponge mat, then release them. Create the next shade of pink by adding the medium pink to white sugar paste in a ratio of 50/50. Repeat the process to create 100 pale pink blossoms. Repeat the process to create 100 white blossoms.

Allow the blossoms to dry and then arrange on the top of the cake in a cross design. The colors can be random among the three shades. When you are happy with the design, glue in place with edible glue. Glue the 3 colored blossoms around the base of the cake in an alternating pattern.

engagement ring box cake

see variations page 62

Say it with cake! What better way to ask someone to marry you?

sugar paste in yellow, white, and pale blue
gold edible luster spray
edible gel diamond
2-layer 2 x 2 1/2-in. sponge cake (page 12)

equipment
cone tool or blade tool

Mix pale yellow sugar paste by adding a small amount of yellow to white sugar paste, or use yellow food coloring paste. Roll out the pale yellow sugar paste to 1/10 in. thick and cut a long 2 1/4 x 1/4-in. strip. Loop the strip and join the ends to create a teardrop shape. Using the same color sugar paste, cut a 1/4 x 1/4-in. square and indent the center with a cone tool to create the mounting for the diamond. You can also indent the edges with a blade tool to create a pattern. Glue the mounting to the top of the ring. Allow to dry for 24 hours and spray with gold edible luster spray. Once dry, glue the edible gel diamond into the mounting.

To create the ring box, cover the sponge cake with white sugar paste. Roll out the pale blue sugar paste to 1/4 in. thick and cut out the following. Base: 2 sides (2 1/2 x 1 3/4 in.); 2 ends (3 x 1 3/4 in.). Lid: 1 top (2 1/2 x 2 in.); 2 sides (2 1/2 x 1 1/4 in.); 2 ends (2 x 1 1/4 in.). Allow the parts to dry for 1 hour before assembling and gluing the lid together. Glue the sides of the box around the cake. Allow to dry for 24 hours. Add white sugar paste ribbon and bow. Indent the top of the cake with a skewer and carefully cut the ring to fit the holes.

baby shower onesie cupcakes

see variations page 63

These cute little cupcake toppers will add an air of festivity to your baby shower.

cupcakes baked in pale pink or pale blue
   cupcake liners (page 16)
3 tbsp. buttercream per cupcake (page 19)
sugar paste in white, light pink, and light blue

equipment
small onesie cutter or template
1/4-in. circle cutter

Roll out the white sugar paste to 1/10 in. thick. Cut out the onesie using a cutter or cut around the template with a craft knife. Roll out the baby pink and baby blue sugar paste to 1/10 in thick. Cut out 1/4-in. circles from both colors, allowing roughly 8 circles per onesie. Take 2 of the circles and cut them in half.

Arrange the baby pink and baby blue circles on the onesie. Create a spotted pattern using the semicircles at the edges. When you are happy with the arrangement, glue the spots in place. Indent the bottom of the onesie with the circle cutter and prick 3 "snaps" using a toothpick.

Repeat until you have the desired number of toppers. Leave them to dry and then place each on top of a frosted cupcake.

silhouette wedding cake & cupcake tower

see variations page 64

Simple, but very elegant, this wedding cake set will delight your nearest and dearest.

6-in. cake covered with white sugar paste
(pages 12, 20)
cupcakes baked in black liners (page 16)
3 tbsp. buttercream per cupcake (page 19)
black sugar paste

equipment
paper, pencil, and scissors
blade tool
2-in. heart cutter
20-in. black ribbon

Using paper and pencil, draw your bride and groom so they resemble the actual people's features and are the correct size for the top of the cake. Ensure the faces are looking at each other and are the same height. Using scissors, cut out the templates. Roll out the black sugar paste to 1/3 in. thick and carefully cut around the templates using a craft knife. Tidy up the edges with a blade tool and smooth the surface with a cake smoother or your fingers.

Insert a toothpick from the bottom, about halfway up. Allow to dry flat for a minimum of 48 hours or until the toppers are completely hard. For the heart cupcake toppers, roll out the black sugar paste to 1/4 in. and cut out the desired number of 2-in. hearts. Lay flat and allow to dry for at least 24 hours. Place a heart on top of each frosted cupcake, elevated at the back, so they can be seen when the cupcakes are on a stand.

Carefully insert the silhouette toppers into the top of the cake. Place a black ribbon around the base of the cake and secure at the back with a pin.

brush embroidery cake

see variations page 65

Delicate flowers outlined over a pale background, this is indeed a very refined cake.

2-layer cake covered with champagne-colored
    sugar paste (pages 12, 20)
white royal icing

equipment
greaseproof paper and pencil
piping bag
Wilton no. 2 tip
square-tip paintbrush
Wilton no. 1 tip
thin, champagne-colored ribbon

Start by drawing your design on greaseproof paper. While your cake is freshly covered, gently lay your design over the cake and lightly imprint it onto the sugar paste with a modeling tool.

Fit the piping bag with a Wilton no. 2 tip and fill with royal icing. Start by piping the outline of a flower. Using the square-tip paintbrush, which should be damp, but not too wet, drag lines of royal icing inward toward the center of the flower. Use this same technique with the leaves, again starting with the outline and pulling toward the center of the leaf.

The center detailing of the leaves and flowers can be piped on with the Wilton no. 1 tip. Use the Wilton no. 2 tip for the vines. Only pipe a small part of the design at a time so the royal icing doesn't have time to set before you start brushing.

Continue until the whole cake is covered. Allow to dry and finish with a thin ribbon around the bottom of each layer.

white lace wedding cake

see variations page 66

Any bride and groom would be delighted to celebrate their wedding with this simply stunning cake.

white sugar paste
6-in. + 8-in. cake, stacked and covered with
    white sugar paste (pages 12, 20, 23)

equipment
selection of flower and leaf cutters
white ribbon

Roll out the sugar paste to 1/10 in. thick. Try to keep to the same thickness throughout. Cut out a selection of sugar paste flowers and leaves in various sizes.

Start by placing some of the larger flowers on the bottom layer and filling in the gaps between them with smaller flowers and leaves.

Continue to add flowers until the cake is completely covered. Allow to dry and finish with a thin white ribbon around the base of each layer.

gerbera wedding cupcakes

see variations page 67

These cupcakes are a good choice for a large wedding party; the flowers are easy to repeat and they look stunning en masse.

cupcakes baked in silver liners (page 16)
2 tbsp. buttercream per cupcake (page 19)
white sugar paste
pearl sprinkles

equipment
2 1/2-in.-wide daisy or gerbera plunger cutter
1-in.-wide daisy cutter
ball tool
piping bag
Wilton 1M tip

Roll out the white sugar paste to 1/4 in. thick. Allow the sugar paste to dry for 5 minutes, which will help it release from the cutter. If you are using a 5-petal daisy cutter, cut two flowers per gerbera, gluing one on top of the other. If you are using a gerbera plunger cutter, you need just one flower per gerbera.

Cut a daisy using the smaller daisy cutter and glue to the center of the gerbera. Indent the center of the gerbera with a ball tool and glue the pearl sprinkles to the center in a flower pattern. Repeat the process for each cupcake. Allow to dry for at least 24 hours.

Pipe the buttercream onto the cupcakes in a swirl pattern, creating a peak. Carefully place a gerbera on top of each cupcake. If you intend to display the cupcakes on a stand, place the gerbera on its side, facing forward for presentation.

new home cupcakes

see variations page 68

A sweet way to wish someone luck in their new home. Customize the decoration to match their new home, if you like!

cupcakes baked in green liners (page 16)
1 tbsp. buttercream per cupcake (page 19)
sugar paste in white, brown, black, blue, and
    green

equipment
house template
blade tool

Roll out the white sugar paste to 1/10 in. thick. Use the template to cut out a house shape with a craft knife. Use the blade tool to make the board effect. Cut rectangles for the window frames and doorframes, and glue in place on the house.

Roll out the brown sugar paste, and cut strips for the roof and rectangles for the front door, window box, and flowerpot. Glue in place on the house. Roll out the black sugar paste and cut out small black rectangles for the windows. Glue in place on the house. Glue some green sugar paste in the flowerpot and window box, and use the end of a craft knife to texture the greenery. Add small spots of white sugar paste as flowers. Repeat the process for each cupcake.

To flat ice the cupcakes, roll pale blue fondant with green at the base and cut a 2 in. circle. Place a tablespoon of buttercream in the center of a cupcake and lay the disc on top. Smooth with the palm of your hand. Leave the houses to dry and glue on top of the flat-iced cupcakes.

golden wedding anniversary cake

see variations page 69

A special anniversary deserves a show-stopping cake and this lavishly decorated two-tier cake certainly fits the bill.

6-in. + 8-in. cake, stacked and covered with
    white sugar paste (pages 12, 20, 23)
gold edible balls
sugar paste in light brown and white
vegetable oil
gold edible paint

equipment
piece of card the depth of the bottom layer of
    cake, cut at a 45° angle
quilting or blade tool
scalloped and plain oval cutters
number cutters
damask pattern mold
paintbrush

When the bottom layer is freshly covered, mark out 1 1/4-in. intervals along the bottom of the cake. Take the piece of card and, using a quilting or blade tool, mark lines along the cake. Continue until covered, then reverse the card and mark around the cake again. Glue gold balls at the intersection of the lines.

Using the scalloped oval cutter, cut a light brown sugar-paste oval. Using a plain oval cutter, cut a white sugar-paste oval. Use number cutters to cut the "50" from light brown sugar paste. Arrange the plaque and affix to the cake.

Before you start the top layer, try photocopying your mold and cutting out the pattern so that you know how to arrange it on the cake and how many of each piece of the pattern to make.

Lightly spray or rub vegetable oil over the mold to prevent sticking. Wipe away any excess. Place the teddy bear sugar paste in the mold and gently press into place. Remove any excess sugar paste from the back of the mold and turn out the shape. Gently glue the parts of the pattern in place to complete the top layer. Use the edible paint to paint all of the light brown sugar paste gold.

variations

new-baby teddy bear mini cupcakes

see base recipe page 41

3-d new-baby teddy bear mini cupcakes

You can use a purchased teddy bear silicone mold to create a 3-D cupcake topper. Brush the inside of the mold with a small amount of vegetable oil and wipe away the excess. Add any details in a contrasting-color sugar paste and then add the main sugar paste to the mold. Turn out of the mold and allow to dry for 24 hours before adding to the top of a flat-iced or frosted cupcake.

flat-iced new-baby teddy bear mini cupcakes

Flat ice a mini cupcake with light brown sugar paste. Add a bear's face by creating a snout, ears, nose, and mouth using sugar paste and imprinting with a craft knife.

"furry" new-baby teddy bear mini cupcakes

Use a Wilton star tip to cover a cupcake with chocolate buttercream to create a fur effect. Mold eyes, ears, nose, and mouth from black sugar paste.

new baby bear-face mini cupcakes

Using a similar technique as the tiger cupcake on page 271, create a bear face cupcake. Cut a 2-in. circle from light brown sugar paste and add the same facial details as the teddy bear mini cupcakes, with snout, ears, mouth, nose, and black eyes made from sugar paste. Allow to dry for 24 hours and place on top of a frosted cupcake.

variations

christening cross cake

see base recipe page 43

flower outline christening cross cake
Inverse the cross design so the blossoms create the outline of the cross and spread away from it in a random pattern.

christening cross cake with daisies
Glue small yellow pearl sprinkles in the center of white-only blossoms to create small daisies for an alternative flower effect.

flower number cake
Use the same effect for a number birthday such as "1," "18," or "21."

fortieth anniversary blossom cake
Create a ruby fortieth anniversary cake by making small blossoms with red sugar paste, and arranging as the numbers "40."

valentine's flower cake
Use red sugar paste to make the blossoms, and arrange in a heart shape.

variations

engagement ring box cake

see base recipe page 44

heart-shaped engagement ring box cake
To create a heart-shaped ring box, cut the cake in the shape of a heart and cover with white sugar paste. Use the same technique to make the box from red sugar paste.

marriage proposal cake
Add a label made from white sugar paste. Allow to dry and write "Will you marry me?" using an edible pen.

engagement ring cake topper
Create the same ring box, but make entirely out of sugar paste to create a cake topper that can be placed on a larger engagement celebration cake.

chocolate box cake
Use the same technique to create a larger box made out of dark brown sugar paste. Add chocolates to the center of the cake to create a box of chocolates.

engagement ring cupcake toppers
Using the same technique, create engagement cupcake toppers by making individual rings topped with edible gel diamonds.

variations

baby shower onesie cupcakes

see base recipe page 47

baby name cupcakes
Remove the spots and use royal icing to pipe the baby's name or surname.

baby motif cupcakes
Add a small teddy bear or duck and coordinate with neutral tones like light brown and yellow.

baby shower patterned onesie cupcakes
Use printed sugar-paste sheets for a patterned effect like gingham.

baby shower detailed onesie cupcakes
Use a craft knife to add stitching details and add sugar-paste buttons.

baby shower cookie favors
Use any of the above designs to decorate a shortbread cookie. A perfect favor for a baby shower.

new baby cake
Create a paper template of a onesie large enough to top a 6-inch cake covered in white sugar paste. Place over pink or blue sugar paste, and cut out. Add the baby's name in stamped letters across the chest of the onesie.

variations

silhouette wedding cake & cupcake tower

see base recipe page 48

entwined heart wedding cake & cupcake tower
Change the silhouettes into 2 entwined hearts; simply alter the stencil before cutting out.

initial silhouette wedding cake & cupcake tower
Use the same technique to create toppers in the bride's and groom's initials or purchase diamante cake initial toppers.

theme-colored silhouette wedding cake & cupcake tower
Create smaller bride and groom silhouettes and add to a sugar-paste plaque in the wedding theme colors. Add to the top of a frosted cupcake.

silhouette cookie wedding favors
Create cookie wedding favors with the black sugar-paste bride and groom silhouettes attached to the tops of shortbread cookies. Place in cellophane bags and tie with a coordinating ribbon.

paper silhouette cupcake toppers
Create a simple cupcake topper by printing the silhouette, cutting it out, and attaching to a lollipop stick. Insert into the top of a frosted cupcake.

variations

brush embroidery cake

see base recipe page 51

sparkly brush embroidery cake
To add more color, brush edible luster dust over the flowers before starting the brush effect.

gilded brush embroidery cake
Paint over the brush embroidery with gold edible paint.

3-d brush embroidery cake
To achieve a more 3-D effect, go over the outline again with a second layer of piped royal icing after the brushing stage.

mother's day brush embroidery cake
Use colored royal icing to create beautiful flowers. Perfect for a birthday or Mother's Day cake.

brush embroidery cookies & cupcakes
Use the brush embroidery effect to decorate sugar paste–covered cookies or flat-iced cupcakes.

variations

white lace wedding cake

see base recipe page 52

flower-topped white lace wedding cake
Add a large floral paste flower to the top of the cake to give it a more vintage feel.

colored lace cake
Use brightly colored flowers to change the feel of the cake, making it suitable for a birthday.

white lace christening cake
Pick cutters to suit the occasion. Use the same effect with baby carriages, teddy bears, bottles, and bibs.

3-d white lace wedding cake
Let the flowers dry in molding cups before adding them to the cake to give a more 3-D feel.

white lace wedding favors
Use the same technique to decorate cupcakes and cookie favors.

lace overlay wedding cake
First, cover the cake with colored sugar paste in place of the white. Proceed as main project.

bubble cake
Substitute pastel-colored sugar paste for the white sugar paste. Replace the flower motifs with circles of different sizes. Affix randomly across the cake.

variations

gerbera wedding cupcakes

see base recipe page 55

gerbera wedding cake

You can use the same gerbera flowers as decoration around the side of a larger cake. This is ideal for a top-cutting cake, which you can use on top of a cupcake tower and display the gerbera cupcakes below.

sparkly gerbera wedding cupcakes

To add some sparkle to the gerberas, glue edible or gel diamonds to the centers of the flowers instead of the pearl sprinkles.

wedding-theme colored gerbera cupcakes

The gerbera color can easily be changed to match any wedding-theme color or celebration. They work well with warm summer colors like hot pink and orange. Add a black sugar-paste center and mark a crosshatch pattern with a craft knife.

sunflower wedding cupcakes

To create sunflowers, cut 2 gerberas from yellow sugar paste and glue together. Add a larger center in either chocolate or black sugar paste marked with a crosshatch pattern. Place on top of a cupcake and place in a terracotta pot for an interesting display.

daisy cupcakes

To create daisies, simply replace the small daisy in the center with a yellow circle.

variations

new home cupcakes

see base recipe page 56

new home message cupcakes
Use the template to cut the house shape from colored sugar paste. Omit the detail on the house, and instead glue contrasting-colored letters on each house to spell "New Home."

house of cupcakes
Use a texture mat to create a brick effect, and flat-ice the cupcakes. Arrange the cupcakes to look like a house, adding sugar-paste doors and windows.

new home silhouette cupcakes
Cut a basic house shape from sugar paste and cut out windows and doors (omitting the sugar-paste color details). Place on a contrasting-color flat-iced cupcake.

multicolored new home cupcakes
Cut sugar-paste houses in different colors and use royal icing to pipe doors and windows.

new home cake
Make a larger house from sugar paste and place on top of an iced cake.

new job cupcakes
Cut out briefcase, tie, or pen shapes from colored sugar paste and place on top of frosted cupcakes.

variations

golden wedding anniversary cake

see base recipe page 58

black-and-white wedding cake
Adapt the design for a striking wedding cake with black damask on a white cake, and change the number plaque for initials.

golden wedding anniversary cupcakes
Use the quilting effect and gold balls to decorate a flat-iced cupcake.

damask cupcake topper
Use part of the damask mold set to create an edible topper for a frosted cupcake.

quick golden wedding anniversary cake
Use royal icing and a stencil on the top tier to create a similar feel in less time.

number plaque birthday cupcakes
Use the number plaque to decorate cupcakes for a number birthday.

silver wedding anniversary cake
Use black and white sugar paste to make a light gray. Use to replace all of the brown sugar paste in the main project. Paint all pieces with edible silver luster paint, and replace gold dragees and ribbon with silver ones. Change the number on the plaque to "25."

birthdays

Show how much you care with a birthday cake

tailor-made for the birthday boy or girl. Whether

they are into golf or shoes, gardening or cupcakes,

there's something for everyone in this chapter.

car cupcakes

see variations page 99

Small children (and, sometimes, not-so-small adults!) love cars, so this is a great choice for birthday cupcakes.

cupcakes baked in bright liners (page 16)
2 tbsp. buttercream per cupcake (page 19)
sugar paste in yellow, white, black, and blue

equipment
paper, pen, and scissors
2 1/4-in. round cutter
1/2-in. round cutter
star tool

Create a car template by drawing a 1 1/2 x 2-in. car shape and cutting it out. Roll out the yellow sugar paste to 1/4 in. thick. Lay the template on the sugar paste and cut it out using a craft knife. Roll out the white sugar paste to 1/10 in. thick and cut out a circle using a 2 1/4-in. circle cutter. Cut the circle into quarters to create the car windows. Glue in place.

Roll the black sugar paste to 1/10 in. thick and cut out 2 wheels using a 1/2-in. round cutter. Roll out a small ball of blue sugar paste 1/4 in. wide for each wheel and press to the center of the wheel. Press with a star tool to form the center of the wheel. Cut a thin strip from the black sugar paste to create the door join and glue in place. Create a small ball of black sugar paste and glue as the door handle. You can repeat this process using different colors of sugar paste and changing the design of the car and its accessories. Allow to dry for 24 hours and place on frosted cupcakes.

balloon cupcakes

see variations page 100

These fun little toppers don't require any special equipment at all, so they're a great first project to build up confidence.

cupcakes baked in primary-color
   liners (page 16)
3 tbsp. buttercream per cupcake (page 19)

sugar paste in yellow, green, and white
red licorice laces

To mold a round balloon, take a 1-in. ball of yellow sugar paste and press gently. Mold the balloon shape, smoothing the surface with your finger. Pinch a small amount of yellow sugar paste between your fingers to create the tied-off end of the balloon. Indent with a toothpick. To mold a long balloon, take a 1 1/4-in. ball of green sugar paste and roll into a sausage shape, smoothing the surface with your finger. Create a green tied end as above. Repeat the process to make additional balloons. You can create alternative color and shaped balloons to complement these cupcakes.

Roll out the white sugar paste to 1/10 in. thick and, using a craft knife, cut out small triangles. Glue these to the top right-hand corner of each balloon to create the reflection. Allow to dry for 24 hours and place the balloons on a frosted cupcake. Add a small cutting of red lace licorice to the base of each balloon to create the balloon's ribbon, and add the tied end at the join.

spot cake

see variations page 101

If you find the lines of spots hard to keep straight, go for a polka-dot motif with randomly colored spots.

2-layer cake covered with white sugar paste
    (pages 12, 20)
sugar paste in yellow, pink, green, and blue

equipment
1/2-in. circle cutter
measuring tape
pin

Lay the measuring tape across the center of the cake, and all the way down each side to the bottom of the cake, and use a pin to prick the center of each spot in the first row. Space the pin pricks every 1 1/2 in. along the measuring tape. Move the tape 1/2 in. down, and 1 1/2 in. across, and repeat the process for each row.

Roll out each color of sugar paste to 1/8 in. thick, and cut out at least 40 circles of each color with the circle cutter. Using the pin pricks as a guide and starting on top of the cake, begin to fix the circles in place with edible glue. When the top of the cake is completed, start fixing the spots on the sides, working down from where the lines finish.

Continue to add the spots until you have completely covered the cake. If you're not happy with the bottom finish of your cake, attach a ribbon to the bottom before you add the spots.

building block cupcakes

see variations page 102

Here's a cake topper for all the construction-lovers in your life.

cupcakes baked in green liners
(page 16)
3 tbsp. buttercream per cupcake (page 19)
sugar paste in red and green
green sugar

equipment
1/4-in. circle cutter
paintbrush

Roll out the red sugar paste to 1/2 in. thick and cut out a rectangular brick. Roll out the red again to 1/10 in. thick and cut out 8 circles with the 1/4-in. circle cutter. Roll out the green sugar paste to 1/4 in. thick and cut out a rectangular brick. Roll out the green again to 1/10 in. thick and cut 6 circles with the 1/4-in. circle cutter. Glue the circles evenly in place on the bricks.

Repeat, using different colored sugar pastes, until you have 24 bricks. Leave the bricks to dry and then place two on each frosted cupcake, sprinkled with green sugar.

cupcake cupcakes

see variations page 103

What do you bake for the baker in your life? Why, a cupcake cupcake, of course!

cupcakes baked in brown liners (page 16)
1 tbsp. buttercream per cupcake (page 19)
sugar paste in red, white, blue, green, and
    dark brown
small, colored chocolate-coated candies

equipment
2 1/2-in. round cutter
blade tool
1 1/4-in. round cutter

Make pastel pink sugar paste by mixing a small amount of the red sugar paste with the white. Repeat the process to create pale blue and pale green sugar paste. Roll out each pastel sugar paste and cut out circles using a 2 1/2-in. round cutter. Add 1 tablespoon of buttercream to the top of a cupcake and place a pastel sugar-paste round on top. Smooth with the palm of your hand. Repeat in varying pastel shades to cover the desired number of cupcakes.

Roll out the dark brown sugar paste to 1/10 in. thick and, using a craft knife, cut out a cupcake liner shape (3/4 in. at the base and 1 1/4 in. at the top). Using a blade tool or craft knife, indent the cupcake liner vertically to create a concertina effect. Glue onto the top of the cupcake.

Roll out the pink sugar paste to 1/10 in. and cut out a circle using a 1 1/4-in. round cutter. Using a craft knife, cut the base of the cupcake frosting in a swirl pattern. This should be half the size of the circle. Glue to the top of the cupcake liner. Glue a colored chocolate-coated candy as the cherry on the top. Repeat the process for each cupcake.

painted shoes cake

see variations page 104

Don't dry the shoes flat or they'll break when you try to glue them in place. Instead, allow a few extra hours to let them dry out once in position.

8-in. cake covered in champagne-colored
    sugar paste (pages 12, 20)
sugar paste in light brown and black
brown food coloring paste
white alcohol

equipment
shoe cutter or template
paintbrush
black edible pen
2-in.-wide black ribbon

Roll out the light brown sugar paste to 1/10 in. thick and cut out about 10 shoes using a shoe cutter or template. Using a craft knife, cut the heel and the sole away, keeping these bits for later. Repeat this process with the black sugar paste, then replace the heel and sole of the shoes with the opposite color heel and sole. Affix in place with some edible glue.

Starting at the bottom of the cake, glue the first row of shoes in place, alternating the two designs. Cut a long, 1/4-in.-wide black sugar-paste strip and glue around the cake. Continue to add the shoes around the top row until completed, then allow to dry.

Mix some brown food coloring paste with some white alcohol, and paint small splotches over the light brown parts of the shoes. Allow to dry. Using a black edible pen, finish the leopard print design. Tie the ribbon into a bow and arrange on top of the cake.

charm bracelet cake

see variations page 105

Perfect for ladies of all ages, a charm bracelet cake is an elegant centerpiece for a sophisticated birthday tea party.

8-in. sponge cake covered with aquamarine
    sugar paste (pages 12, 20)
sugar paste in black, white, blue, and green
silver edible luster spray

equipment
1 1/4-in. circle cutters
small flower, star, and heart cutters
satin ribbon

Mix gray sugar paste by adding a small amount of black sugar paste to white. Also mix an accent color to match the color of the cake. Make aquamarine sugar paste by mixing a small amount of blue and green sugar paste. Mold a range of individual charms out of the gray sugar paste. These can be achieved by using 1 1/4-in. circle, small flower, star, and heart cutters. Some can be discs decorated with indent patterns or flowers. Others can be ball-shaped and pricked with a skewer to create a dimpled effect. Remember to include some aspects of the accent aquamarine color.

Create the main heart charm by using a 2 1/4-in. heart cutter and attaching two small ball joints with edible glue. To create a letter charm, use an alphabet cutter or cut by freehand.

Let the charms dry for 24 hours, then spray with silver edible luster spray. Once dry, arrange the charms on a flat surface. When you are happy with the design, glue to the top of the cake with edible glue. Secure a coordinating satin ribbon around the base of the cake.

cosmetic cupcakes

see variations page 106

These will go down a storm with ladies who like to look their best!

cupcakes baked in black liners (page 16)
3 tbsp. buttercream per cupcake (page 19)
sugar paste in pink, black, and gold
gold edible luster dust

equipment
clear alcohol
paintbrush

Create a pink sugar-paste sausage and cut one end at a 45-degree angle to create the lipstick. Use the black sugar paste to mold a cube for the base of the lipstick and an oblong shape for the lipstick lid. Use the gold sugar paste to mold a smaller block for the base of the lipstick.

Glue the pink lipstick, gold base, and black base together, and leave to dry. Mix the gold luster dust with some clear alcohol to create edible paint, and paint the gold section of the lipstick. Repeat the process until you have one lipstick for each cupcake.

Leave to dry and then place one on top of each frosted cupcake, leaning against the lipstick lid.

rain boot cupcakes

see variations page 107

These rain boots also look cute arranged along the base of a large cake, with the top covered in crushed cookies (to represent earth) and a selection of the sugar paste vegetables and garden tools from the vegetable crate project on page 92.

cupcakes baked in green liners (page 16)
3 tbsp. buttercream per cupcake (page 19)
sugar paste in green, gray, yellow, and red
silver edible luster dust

equipment
boot cutter or template
clear alcohol

Roll out the green sugar paste and cut out the boot using the boot cutter or template. Cut two strips to make the boot straps and cut one end into a point. Roll out the gray sugar paste. Cut out gray strips to create the buckle and glue in place. Allow to dry. Mix some clear alcohol with the silver luster dust and use it to paint the silver buckle.

Repeat the process until you have the desired number of rain boots. Use yellow and red sugar paste to make contrasting color rain boots. Allow to dry and then place one boot on each frosted cupcake.

eighteenth-birthday popcorn bucket cake

see variations page 108

One for the teenage movie fan, this looks much more complicated than it really is. To make the soda-cup and mini popcorn cakes, see instructions on page 108.

two 6 x 4 x 2.5-in. pound cakes
jelly for filling
buttercream for light covering and center
    (page 19)
sugar paste in red and white
mini white marshmallows

equipment
serrated knife
3/4-in. circle cutter
2-in. serrated oval cutter
number cutters
scissors

Sandwich the pound cakes together with a thin layer of jelly and buttercream. Place in the freezer for 30 minutes. Remove the cake from the freezer and stand on its end. Using a serrated kitchen knife, carve the popcorn box shape. It is less likely to crumble if slightly frozen. The top of the box should be 4 in. square and the base roughly 3 1/4 in. square. Once you are happy with the shape, cover the cake with a thin layer of buttercream to act as glue for the sugar paste.

Roll out the white sugar paste to 1/4 in. thick and cut 6 1/2-in.-long strips, starting at 3/4 in. wide and tapering to 1 1/4 in. wide at the base. At the top, imprint the 3/4-in. circle cutter and use the craft knife to cut out the semicircle top. You will need approximately 12 white strips. Repeat the process with red sugar paste.

Attach the strips to the cake, smoothing with your fingers to secure. You may need extra glue for the sugar-paste strips to adhere to each other. Repeat until all sides are covered.

To create a rosette, cut a red sugar-paste oval and a white sugar-paste oval using the 2-in. serrated oval cutter. Use number cutters for the red "18." Glue together and attach to the front of the box. Using the scissors, snip the marshmallows with a cross to create the popcorn. Place the popcorn on top of the cake and secure with edible glue, if needed.

handbag cupcakes

see variations page 109

The handles on these bags are quite delicate, and may break once dried; make extra just in case.

cupcakes baked in black liners (page 16)
3 tbsp. buttercream per cupcake (page 19)
vegetable oil
sugar paste in black and cream
black food coloring paste
white alcohol
gold edible luster dust

equipment
handbag mold
paintbrush

Lightly spray or rub vegetable oil over the mold to prevent sticking. Wipe away any excess. Gently place the black sugar paste in the mold where the buckle and straps will be. Place the cream sugar paste in the rest of the mold and gently press into place. Allow to dry and then turn out the mold.

Mix some black food coloring paste with some white alcohol and paint a zebra pattern on the bag. Mix some gold edible luster dust with the alcohol and paint the gold detailing.

Repeat the process until you have one handbag for each cupcake. Allow to dry and then place one on each frosted cupcake.

vegetable crate cake

see variations page 110

Perfect for all gardening enthusiasts! You can create endless different combinations of vegetables to fill the crate cake.

8-in. square sponge cake
10 tbsp. buttercream for thin covering
   (page 19)
sugar paste in light brown, dark brown, orange,
   green, white, and red
crushed Oreo crumbs

equipment
black edible pen
blade tool
ball tool

Create wood-effect sugar paste by rolling a small sausage of light brown sugar paste and adding it to a larger sausage of dark brown sugar paste. Press together and then fold together, twist, and fold together again. Repeat until the grain effect appears. Roll out the sugar paste to 1/4 in. thick and cut out a 21 x 2-in. rectangle. Repeat to create 8 wooden boards. Lay flat and allow to dry for 24 hours. Once dry, use a black edible pen to write the desired name on in a stencil fashion.

Cover the cake with a thin layer of buttercream to act as glue, and add the boards, 2 on each side, until the cake is encased.

Use different colors of sugar paste to mold a selection of vegetables to place in the crate. Make carrots by molding orange sugar paste and using a blade tool or craft knife to indent the shaft with horizontal lines. Add a green sugar-paste sprout on the top. Make scallions or leeks by joining pale green and white sugar paste and forming a sausage shape. Add strips of

green sugar paste as outer leaves. Make potatoes by adding a small amount of light brown to white sugar paste, and using a ball tool to add blemishes to the potatoes. Roll in black Oreo crumbs to look like newly dug potatoes. Radishes are red sugar-paste balls with white sugar-paste tips and a green sugar-paste sprig on top.

Allow vegetables to dry, then lay on top of the cake. Secure with edible glue, if needed.

fishing cake

see variations page 111

The fishing line isn't edible; remember to remove it before serving.

8-in. cake covered in pale green sugar paste
(pages 12, 20)
sugar paste in bottle green, black, white, brown,
pink, light green, red, gray, orange and blue

equipment
4 3/4-in. round cutter
2-in. round cutter
4-in. polystyrene craft ball
blade tool
short length of silver embroidery thread

To create the fishing umbrella, roll out the bottle green sugar paste to 1/4 in. thick and use the 4 3/4-in. round cutter to cut out a circle. Use the 2-in. round cutter to cut out the edges around the sides. Mold the umbrella onto the polystyrene ball, and use a craft knife or blade tool to indent the frame of the umbrella.

To make the tackle box, mold a rectangular box from the bottle green sugar paste. Mold a thinner white sugar-paste rectangle to form the tackle box lid. Add a black sugar-paste handle and latch to the tackle box. To form the sandwich box, create another small bottle green rectangle. Mold the sandwiches by making white bread, pink ham, light green lettuce, and red tomatoes out of sugar paste. Wrap brown and gray sugar paste around one skewer, and affix the embroidery thread to represent the rod and line. Make a handle from black sugar paste. Mold a duck's body from light brown sugar paste and add two wings. Roll a light green sugar-paste head and add an orange sugar-paste bill. Indent the tail and eyes with a toothpick. To create the stones, add a small amount of black to white sugar paste and mix until you have a marble effect. Mold small, uneven stones about 1/2 in. wide. Allow all of these sugar paste components to dry for at least 24 hours.

Make water-effect sugar paste by folding white and blue sugar paste repeatedly. Roll it flat to 1/4 in. and then cut out the river and waterfall. Attach to the cake using edible glue. Insert the skewer where you want to place the umbrella, and attach the umbrella with a small ball of sugar paste and glue. Glue the remaining parts to the cake and add the stones around the base of the cake and around the river.

birthday brooch cake

see variations page 112

Spectacular and dramatic, the elements of this cake can all be prepared well in advance of the birthday celebration, and it's quick to assemble at the last minute.

3 sponge cakes: 8-in., 6-in., and 4-in. (page 12)
2 x quantity buttercream (page 19)
sugar paste in white, blue, and black
1 tsp. vegetable oil
pearl ball sprinkles
baby blue metallic food paint

equipment
1 3/4-in.-wide brooch silicone mold
8-in., 6-in., and 4-in. round cake boards
8 cake stacking dowels
3/4-in. wide aquamarine ribbon
pearl-topped pins
diamante number cake topper
black craft feathers

Create baby blue sugar paste by mixing 2 teaspoons of white with 1 teaspoon of blue sugar paste, or use blue food paste. Lightly paint the inside of the silicone mold with vegetable oil to prevent the sugar paste from sticking. Press a ball of baby blue sugar paste into the oval section of the mold and add 4 pearl ball sprinkles to corner enclaves (if included).

Cover the rest of the mold with black sugar paste, pressing firmly. Cut the excess sugar paste using a knife, flush against the mold. Turn out the mold and repeat to make a total of 3 brooches. Allow to dry for 24 hours, then paint the center oval with baby blue metallic paint to give a gloss effect.

Cover each cake with a thin layer of buttercream and allow to set in the refrigerator for 3 hours, before covering each with white sugar paste (page 20) and allow to dry overnight.

Stack the cakes (page 23) using the cake dowels. Pin the satin ribbon around the base of the 3 layers and secure at the back with pearl-topped pins. Attach the brooches to the front of each cake over the satin ribbon with edible glue and a small ball of white sugar paste. Add the diamante topper and feathers to the top cake.

soccer shirt cupcakes

see variations page 113

Choose sugar paste in the colors of the birthday person's favorite team.

cupcakes baked in green liners (page 16)
3 tbsp. green buttercream per cupcake
    (page 19)
sugar paste in red and white
foil-covered chocolate soccerballs

equipment
paper, pen, and scissors, or 2-in. baby
    onesie cutter
piping bag
Wilton no. 233 grass tip

For the shirt shape, you can create a template using a pen and paper, or a baby onesie cutter, which can double as a shirt shape. Roll out the red sugar paste to 1/10 in. thick and cut out the shirt shape. Roll out the white sugar paste and cut out another shirt shape to create the sleeves. Cut off the sleeves of both shirts and replace the red sleeves with white ones and glue them in place.

Cut the end of the red sleeve and glue to the end of the new white sleeve to create a red trim. Cut a small crest shape from the white sugar paste and glue onto the chest. Allow to dry for 24 hours.

Place the green buttercream into a piping bag with a Wilton no. 233 grass tip. Start to pipe the grass by touching the cupcake, applying pressure, and pulling away. Repeat until the whole cupcake is iced. Add the soccer shirt to the top. Repeat the process for each cupcake. Serve with foil-covered chocolate soccerballs.

car cupcakes

see base recipe page 71

road sign cupcakes

Create a road sign cupcake topper with the child's age on it. Roll out white sugar paste to 1/10 in. thick and cut a 1 1/4-in. circle. Roll out some red sugar paste and cut out another 1 1/4-in. circle. Using a smaller 2 1/4-in. circle, cut out the middle of the red circle and glue the ring to the edge of the white circle. Add a number by using a tappit from black sugar paste or use a black edible pen.

bus cupcakes

Create a bus template using the same technique as for the car. Add white square windows and a door with a black door handle.

tractor cupcakes

Create a template for a tractor and cut out of the sugar paste color of your choice. Create large and small wheels like the car cupcake, and add white windows to the cab. Add a black stripe between the door and window. Add a gray engine between the two wheels.

train cupcakes

Create a train using the same template technique. Add the engine to the front cupcakes and individual carriages to other cupcakes to create a "cupcake train." You could also add different loads to the trucks and even add a child's name.

variations

balloon cupcakes

see base recipe page 72

balloon number cupcakes
Pipe or write the child's age onto a balloon with royal icing (page 19).

hot-air balloon cupcakes
Enlarge the round balloon and create hot-air balloons with a light brown sugar-paste basket below. The balloons can be colorfully decorated with spots, stripes, or small stars.

3-d balloon cupcakes
Mold the balloons and place a small lollipop into the base of the balloon. Allow to dry and insert two balloons into the top of a frosted cupcake, so they are elevated above.

balloon spray cake topper
Mold the same balloon shape and insert floral wire into the base, halfway up the balloon. Repeat at least 8 times. Allow to dry for 24 hours and then insert into the center of a cake.

balloon cake pops
Make balloon-shaped cake pops covered in different primary-color candy melts. Add the white sugar paste reflection, and attach a small piece of red lace licorice to the base and allow to hang down like ribbon.

variations

spot cake

see base recipe page 75

flower cake
Substitute the spots for small flowers made with a plunge cutter.

snowflake cake
Replace the spots with white snowflakes for a beautiful Christmas cake finish. Add a metallic ribbon around the base of the cake.

spot cupcake & cookie favors
Flat-ice cupcakes or cookies with white sugar paste and add the colored spots using the same technique, for party favors.

spot number cake
Use the same technique to create a number cake to celebrate a particular birthday.

spot and stripe cake
Restrict the spot pattern to the top of the cake. Cut long, narrow ribbons of colored sugar paste and fix around the sides of the cake.

rainbow spot cake
Cut the spots from red, orange, yellow, green, blue, and purple colors. Arrange the rows to resemble a rainbow.

variations

building block cupcakes

see base recipe page 76

building board cupcakes
Flat-ice a cupcake with green sugar paste, add a block, and add green circles to the rest of the cupcake to look like a building board.

building block cake
Decorate the top of a large cake with blocks and use the block design to make a border around the base of the cake.

building block-shaped mini cakes
Create mini cakes in the shape of building blocks.

mini figure cupcake toppers
Create sugar-paste mini people such as brides and grooms as cake and cupcake toppers.

building block cake pops
Make block-shaped cake pops.

variations

cupcake cupcakes

see base recipe page 78

cupcake cake
Use the cupcake toppers as decoration around the side of a large round cake.

shaped cupcake cake
Create a large cake shaped like a cupcake, and decorate with the same sugar-paste colors with a large sugar-paste cherry on the top.

giant cupcake cake
Bake a giant cupcake cake and turn the base section upside down and cover with chocolate sugar paste. Trim the top. Allow to harden for 2 hours, then turn over and add the top section. Frost the top with buttercream, and add colored sprinkles and a large sugar-paste cherry on top.

cupcake mosaic
Place baked cupcakes on a cake board in the shape of a cupcake and decorate the top of the cupcakes as one cake. Place chocolate sugar paste over the cupcake liner section and frost the top with buttercream. Decorate with colored sugar-paste discs and a large sugar-paste cherry on the top.

cupcake cake pops
Create cake pops to look like cupcakes with chocolate-coated candy as the cherry on top.

variations

painted shoes cake

see base recipe page 81

painted shoe cupcake topper
Emboss a pattern onto a disc of sugar paste and mount the shoe on the
disc to make a cupcake topper.

sparkly shoe cake
Use a stencil and luster dust to decorate the shoes before placing on the cake.

3-d shoe cake
Make a 3-D shoe from sugar paste and paint the leopard print over the shoe. Place on top of
the cake in place of the ribbon bow.

painted handbag cake
Instead of shoe shapes, cut out handbag shapes. Decorate as directed in the main project.

leopard-print cake
Use the leopard print to paint the whole cake. Great for a jungle-theme party.

animal-print cake
Use the painting technique for other animal prints such as zebra, cheetah,
or giraffe.

variations

charm bracelet cake

see base recipe page 82

pearl necklace cake
Create a pearl necklace or bracelet out of white sugar-paste balls that have been sprayed with edible pearlized luster spray.

ring cake
Create gold and silver rings by spraying with luster sprays and adding edible gel diamonds.

gold charm bracelet cake
Create gold jewelry by molding pale yellow sugar paste and painting with edible gold paint.

tiffany-style charm bracelet
Create a Tiffany-style bracelet by molding gray sugar paste, painting with silver luster paint, and adding a heart charm. Indent with a name.

jewelry box cake
Create a jewelry box cake with a ballerina figurine and candy necklaces. Ideal for a little girl's birthday.

variations

cosmetic cupcakes

see base recipe page 85

eye shadow cupcake topper
Create an eye shadow by making a black sugar-paste square and gluing two different shades of pink sugar paste on top to look like eye shadow. Use black and white sugar paste to form an applicator.

nail polish cupcake topper
Create a nail polish using pink sugar paste for the bottle and black sugar paste for the lid. Paint over with some light silver luster dust and white alcohol to give the bottle a sheen.

mascara cupcake topper
Create a mascara from black sugar paste and use a craft knife to texture the sugar-paste brush.

makeup brush cupcake topper
Create a makeup brush from black sugar paste for the handle and brown for the brush; separate the two with a silver collar. Use a blade tool to indent the brush.

makeup bag cake
Place all of the above together with a makeup bag on top of an 8-inch cake. Mold a makeup bag from black sugar paste and use a craft tool to indent a quilted effect on the bag.

variations

rain boot cupcakes

see base recipe page 86

flowery rain boot cupcakes
Use a stencil and luster to decorate the boot with a floral pattern.

painted rain boot cupcakes
Hand-paint the boot with flowers or an animal print using food coloring paste and clear alcohol.

quilted rain boot cupcakes
Use a quilting tool to add a padded effect to the boot, or use a black and brown leather look for an equestrian lover and add a sugar-paste riding crop.

rain boot cake
Make a larger boot to decorate a large cake for a garden lover. Add crumbled Oreo cookies for dirt, and make flowerpots and flowers from sugar paste.

family rain boot cupcakes
For a family that loves camping or walking, make a boot for each family member and use royal icing to pipe names onto each one.

variations

eighteenth-birthday popcorn bucket cake

see base recipe page 88

popcorn cupcake
Use the same technique to create the popcorn to add to the top of a cupcake, placed in a striped cupcake liner.

cola cupcakes
Create coordinating cola cupcakes by piping chocolate buttercream on top of a cupcake and adding crushed clear mints and white sugar. Add a candy stick as a straw. Place in matching striped cupcake liners.

movie ticket cupcakes
Create movie ticket cupcake toppers by cutting out ticket shapes from rolled red sugar paste. Allow to dry and write "18" and a message of your choice in edible black pen.

popcorn cake pops
Create popcorn-shaped cake pops and insert the cake pop stick into the top of a popcorn bucket.

variations

handbag cupcakes

see base recipe page 91

embossed handbag cupcakes
Emboss a pattern onto sugar paste and cut out a handbag-shaped topper.

sparkly handbag cake
Make a handbag stencil and use to decorate a larger cake. Cover cake topper with luster.

animal print handbag cupcakes
Hand-paint your bag with an animal print using food coloring paste and water.

quilted handbag cupcakes
Use a quilting tool to add a padded effect to a handbag.

flowery handbag cupcakes
Cut small sugar-paste flowers and use them to decorate a handbag topper.

variations

vegetable crate cake

see base recipe page 92

garden plot cake
Create a garden plot cake by covering the top with Oreo crumb dirt and adding the vegetables in rows in the earth. Add sugar-paste accessories such as a spade or watering can.

flower garden
Create a variety of garden flowers from different-colored sugar pastes. Place in Oreo crumb dirt. Make a white sugar-paste picket fence to go around the side of the cake.

vegetable basket cake
Create a vegetable basket cake by piping buttercream around the side of the cake using a Wilton no. 47 basket tip.

vegetable garden cupcakes
Cover frosted cupcakes with Oreo crumb dirt and place a small sugar-paste vegetable on top of each.

carrot cake topper
Create a large carrot cake topper using the same modeling technique as a decoration for a carrot cake or an Easter cake.

variations

fishing cake

see base recipe page 94

sea fishing cake
Create a fishing cake using the same technique, but add a sea at the front using water-effect sugar paste and add graham cracker crumbs for the sand.

fishing message topper
Make a wooden sign with wood-effect sugar paste by folding chocolate sugar paste with light brown. Roll out to 1/2 in. thick and cut out a wooden sign with 2 legs. Attach the legs with toothpicks. Once dry, use an edible pen to write your message, such as "Gone Fishing!" or "Happy Birthday!"

fish cupcake toppers
Create fish cupcake toppers and use a piping tip to indent the scales.

duck cupcake toppers
Create coordinating duck cake toppers by using the same technique to mold the duck. Allow to dry and place on a frosted cupcake.

water-effect buttercream piping
Create water-effect cupcakes by adding white buttercream to a bag with blue buttercream. Use a star tip to create waves on the cupcake in the two-tone frosting. Add fish toppers.

variations

birthday brooch cake

see base recipe page 96

vintage gold brooch cake
Create pale gold sugar paste by mixing a small amount of yellow with white sugar paste. Add ivory sugar paste to the oval section and then the pale gold over the top to the rest of the mold. Once you have turned out the mold, use edible gold luster to paint the brooch gold. Paint the oval section with pearl luster to create a vintage-style brooch.

brooch cupcakes
Roll out baby blue sugar paste and use a 2-in. scalloped-edge round cutter to create a background for the brooch. Attach the brooch with edible glue and allow to dry for 24 hours. Add to the top of a frosted cupcake baked in a baby blue or black cupcake liner.

brooch mini cake
Create gray sugar paste by mixing a small amount of black with white sugar paste. Add to the brooch mold and release. Spray the entire brooch with silver luster spray and allow to dry. Paint the central oval with edible metallic paint in the color of your choice (e.g. pink) and add to the front of a mini cake covered in white sugar paste and secured with a matching satin ribbon.

ruffle brooch cake
Roll out baby blue sugar paste to 1/10 in. thick and cut a long strip about 8 in. long and 1 3/4 in. wide. Gather the strip together in pleats and arrange in a rosette shape. Glue the brooch to the center and add to the side of a cake with a matching satin ribbon.

soccer shirt cupcakes

see base recipe page 98

rugby shirt cupcakes
Change the shape to create a rugby shirt from your favorite team. The sleeves are bigger and squarer, and the shirts tend to have white collars.

american football shirt cupcakes
Change the shape to create an American football shirt. The shirts have V-necks and are larger. You can also add a molded light brown sugar-paste football with edible black pen details.

personalized football shirt cupcakes
Personalize the shirts by piping the name or age onto them with royal icing using a Wilton no. 1 tip. You could do the same with edible pens.

father's day shirt cupcakes
Use the same template or baby onesie cutter to create Father's Day shirts with tie details.

soccer cupcake
Lightly brush a silicone soccerball mold with vegetable oil and wipe away the excess. Add the black details with black sugar paste and then overlay with white sugar paste. Turn out the mold and place on a cupcake covered with green sugar paste or piped green-grass buttercream.

occasions

Cakes are a perfect way to display holiday themes.

Special occasions such as New Year's, Valentines,

and Halloween provide ample opportunities to be

creative, and have lots of fun too!

valentine glittered heart cupcakes

see variations page 138

For an extra-special touch, bake these cupcakes in heart-shaped cases.

cupcakes baked in red liners (page 16)
3 tbsp. chocolate buttercream per cupcake
(page 19)
red sugar paste
red edible glitter

equipment
small heart cutter
paintbrush
piping bag
Wilton 1M tip

Roll out the red sugar paste to 1/4 in. thick. Using the small heart cutter, cut out heart shapes, 1 for each cupcake. Allow to dry for 10 minutes. Brush each heart with edible glue. Place on a separate plate and, using a clean paintbrush, sprinkle each with red edible glitter. Allow hearts to dry for a few hours.

Place the chocolate frosting in a piping bag with a Wilton 1M tip. Starting from the back of the cupcake, swirl the buttercream around the edge, then continue inward to fill. Now pipe a smaller second ring in the center to form a peak. Before the buttercream sets and forms a crust, add the glittered heart to the top of the cupcake.

Sprinkle more red edible glitter all over the cupcake. Repeat the process for each cupcake.

st. patrick's day cupcakes

see variations page 139

They say everyone's Irish on St. Patrick's Day — so get in the spirit with these easy toppers.

cupcakes baked in green liners (page 16)
1 tbsp. buttercream per cupcake (page 19)
sugar paste in green and white

equipment
small heart cutter
1 3/4-in. scalloped-edge circle cutter
2 1/2-in plain circle cutter
piping bag
Wilton 1M tip

Roll out the green sugar paste to 1/10 in. thick. Using a small heart cutter, cut out 3 hearts to form the shamrock leaves. Also cut out the shamrock's stem, 1 1/4 in. long, tapering at one end. Roll out the white sugar paste to 1/4 in. thick and cut out a 1 3/4-in. circle using a scalloped-edge circle cutter to create a background plaque for the shamrock. Glue the 3 shamrock leaves and stem to the center of the white plaque. Cut a 2 1/2-in. circle from the green sugar paste using the plain circle cutter. Repeat for each cupcake.

Spread a tablespoon of buttercream onto each cooled cupcake, and place the green sugar paste on top. Smooth with the palm of your hand to make a flat surface. Glue the shamrock plaque to the center of each cupcake.

easter simnel cake

see variations page 140

Simnel cake, a light, moist fruitcake, is the ultimate Easter treat in the United Kingdom and other countries. The topping is a sweet, pastel-yellow confection that's decorated with marzipan balls, which represent the apostles.

8-in. ready-made simnel fruitcake
18 oz. ready-to-roll marzipan
apricot jam
sugar paste in white, light brown, yellow, and
    orange

equipment
2-in. round cutter
egg cups
1/2-in.-wide heart cutter
black edible pen

Roll out the white sugar paste to 1/10 in. thick and cut out a 2-in. circle using the round cutter. Using a craft knife, cut triangles from the edge to create the "cracked shell" effect. Place the eggshell into an egg cup to form the shape, then remove after 15 minutes. Repeat the process in light brown sugar paste to create brown eggshells.

From the yellow sugar paste, mold the chick's body 2 in. tall with a head and rounded body. Use a 1/2-in.-wide heart cutter, cut in half and glue to the side of the body as wings. Take a small amount of orange sugar paste and mold the chick's mouth in a diamond shape. Indent the center and bend. Glue to the front of the chick's face. Use black edible pen to mark the chick's eyes. Glue the chick into the shell and glue the eggshell's cracked edges to the chick. Repeat the process for the desired number of chicks.

Roll out the marzipan to 1/2 in. thick, and cut around the cake pan you used for the simnel cake. Paint the top of the simnel cake with some warmed apricot jam and then lay the marzipan circle on top.

Roll 12 marzipan balls 1 1/4 in. wide to represent apostles. Place on a baking sheet with parchment paper and place under a medium grill for 1–2 minutes, until lightly toasted. Place the browned apostles around the edge of the cake and secure with edible glue. Place the chicks on top of the simnel cake.

spring bunny cupcakes

see variations page 141

Welcome spring in style with a basket of these delightful bunny-themed cupcakes.

cupcakes baked in brown liners (page 16)
2 tbsp. buttercream per cupcake (page 19)
sugar paste in brown, pink, white, and black
green food coloring paste

equipment
blade tool
piping bag
Wilton no. 233 piping tip

Roll a ball of fondant from the brown sugar paste for the bunny's head. Mold 2 ears from brown sugar paste and add pink sugar paste to the center of the ears. Glue to the head. Mold 2 bunny feet from brown sugar paste and use a blade tool to mark the toes. Craft a snout from the white sugar paste. Indent a mouth and add a pink nose. Use black sugar paste to make the eyes and glue into position. Allow to dry so the ears are lying flat and the head is lying on them.

Add some green food coloring paste to the buttercream and place in a piping bag with a Wilton no. 233 piping tip. Frost the cupcake to look like grass, and place the feet and the head on the cupcake. Repeat the process for each cupcake.

mother's day cupcakes

see variations page 142

Put a smile on mom's face this Mother's Day with these beautiful floral cupcakes.

cupcakes baked in hot pink liners (page 16)
3 tbsp. buttercream per cupcake (page 19)
sugar paste in hot pink and pale green

equipment
small leaf cutter or plunger cutter
cupcake box (optional)
satin hot pink ribbon (optional)

Roll out the hot pink sugar paste to 1/4 in. thick and, using a craft knife, cut out a
1 1/4 x 3/4-in. rectangle. Smooth the top edge with your finger. Starting at one end, roll the
sugar paste between your two fingers, pinching at the base, forming the rosebud. As you
reach the end of the roll, pull the end over the bottom and pinch to create the bud effect.
Repeat the process to create 3 rosebuds per cupcake.

Roll out the pale green sugar paste to 1/4 in. thick and use the small leaf cutter to create the
rose leaf. If you don't have a plunger cutter, which imprints the leaf veins, use a craft knife
to make similar marks. Repeat for additional leaves.

Allow to dry for 24 hours and place on frosted cupcakes. Place the cupcakes in a cupcake
box and tie with a satin hot pink ribbon.

ice-cream cone cupcakes

see variations page 143

Can't decide between an ice cream or a cupcake? Have both! These whimsical cupcakes make the perfect summer treat and are bound to impress.

cupcake batter, unbaked (page 16)   red sugar paste
3 tbsp. buttercream per cupcake (page 19) multicolor nonpareils
store-bought, flat-bottomed ice cream cones

Spoon the cake batter into the ice cream cones, leaving 1/2 in. space at the top. Stand the filled cones on a cupcake baking tray, and carefully transfer to the oven. Bake as directed on page 16. Cool completely before decorating.

Create a red cherry by rolling a ball of red sugar paste 3/4 in. wide. Using a skewer, insert a hole into the top. Create the cherry's stem by rolling a thin sausage of red sugar paste and pinching the end. Ensure that the stem will fit into the hole at the top of the cherry. Place the stem flat in a semicircle shape. Repeat the process for each cupcake. Allow to dry for 24 hours. When dry, insert a stem into the top of each cherry. Use edible glue to fix, if needed.

Frost the top of each cupcake with a double whip to imitate ice cream, and immediately sprinkle with the nonpareils before the frosting crusts. Add a cherry to the top of each frosted cupcake.

summer pinwheel cupcakes

see variations page 144

A sugar sheet is a layer of ready-rolled sugar paste printed with edible food colors. They are available from most cake decorating manufacturers and suppliers.

printed sugar sheets
pink sugar paste
cupcakes baked in pale blue and pale pink
    cupcake liners (page 16)
3 tbsp. buttercream per cupcake (page 19)

equipment
scissors
foam mat
pearl- or ball-head pins

Use scissors to cut out a 2 1/4-in. square from the covered sugar paste. Lightly mark a diagonal cross with craft knife on the back of the sheet so the center is clearly visible. Cut from one corner toward the center, stopping about 1/4 in. from the center. Repeat on the three remaining corners.

Place the square on the foam mat with the pattern facing up. Take the top left corner of the top section and carefully bend the point to the center below. Secure this point with a pin into the mat below. Turn the square 90 degrees and repeat the process until all 4 corners are folded. Repeat the process for each cupcake.

Allow to dry. When the pinwheels have dried, carefully remove the pins and add a pink sugar-paste ball to each center. Allow to dry for 24 hours and place one pinwheel on each frosted cupcake.

star cupcakes

see variations page 145

These are a great way to celebrate any achievement — an exam aced, a successful recital, or MVP in a game.

mini cupcakes baked in gold foil mini liners
(page 16)
2 tbsp. buttercream per cupcake (page 19)
sugar paste in yellow and white
gold edible luster spray
gold edible glitter

equipment
2 1/4-in.-wide star cutter
paintbrush
piping bag
star tip

Mix pale yellow sugar paste by adding a small amount of yellow to white sugar paste. Roll out the pale yellow sugar paste to 1/4 in. thick and use the star cutter to cut out as many stars as are desired. Place stars on a tray covered with parchment paper and spray with gold luster spray. Using a paintbrush, immediately sprinkle the gold glitter onto the stars while the gold spray is still wet. Allow to dry for 24 hours.

Place the buttercream into a piping bag with a star tip and pipe onto the mini cupcakes. Start at the back, then go around the front, and finish with a final swirl in the middle. Place the golden stars on top of the mini cupcakes.

halloween cupcakes

see variations page 146

There are so many halloween themes you can pick for cupcake motifs; the witch's hat is a classic, and there are more of our favorites on page 146.

cupcakes baked in black and orange liners
(page 16)
3 tbsp. buttercream per cupcake (page 19)
sugar paste in black and orange

equipment
paper, pencil, and scissors, or a selection of
small Halloween cutters
paintbrush

Using a pencil and paper, draw a witch's hat template and cut it out. Roll out the black sugar paste to 1/4 in. thick. Place the witch's hat template onto the black sugar paste and cut it out.

Roll out the orange sugar paste and cut out a 3/4 in. x 1/4-in. rectangle to create the witch's hat ribbon. Glue the ribbon around the base of the hat. Repeat the process for each cupcake.

Allow to dry for 24 hours and place on top of frosted cupcakes.

nordic noel cake

see variations page 147

For extra authenticity, make an almond-flavored cake by replacing the vanilla essence with almond essence and replacing an eighth of the flour with ground almonds.

cake covered with white sugar paste
(pages 12, 20)
red sugar paste
white royal icing

equipment
selection of cutters or templates for a bauble,
heart, and circle
piping bag
Wilton no. 1 tip
pinecones

Roll out the red sugar paste to 1/10 in. thick and cut a selection of round, heart, and bauble shapes using a cutter or template.

To create the circle bauble, cut out a circle from the red sugar paste with a 2-in. plain cookie cutter. Cut a star from the center and place over a 2-in. white sugar-paste circle. Fill the piping bag with white royal icing and pipe a pattern onto the red sugar-paste bauble using a mix of diamonds and zigzags. Cut a small heart shape from red sugar paste and affix to the center.

Try cutting out reindeers and snowflakes from white sugar paste and affix in the center of the baubles. When all of the baubles have dried, glue in place around the cake.

Roll out the red sugar paste to 1/10 in. thick and cut 1/4-in.-wide strips for the ribbons. Glue in place. Decorate the top of the cake with pinecones.

christmas tree cupcakes

see variations page 148

These are just so easy to make, and very effective in a group. Make these, and you'll be the star of the holiday bake sale!

cupcakes baked in red liners (page 16)
4 tbsp. green buttercream per cupcake
    (page 19)
yellow sugar paste
multicolor disc sprinkles

equipment
1 1/4-in. star cutter
piping bag
Wilton 1M tip

Roll out the yellow sugar paste to 1/10 in. thick and cut out a star for each cupcake using the 1 1/4-in. star cutter. Allow the stars to dry for 24 hours.

Place the buttercream in a piping bag with a Wilton 1M tip and start the swirl at the back to the front of the cupcake. Create the Christmas tree height by piping 4 layers, gradually getting smaller and finishing with the tip.

Before the buttercream can crust, immediately add the disc sprinkles sporadically around the Christmas tree. Place the yellow star on the top of the Christmas tree. Repeat the process for each cupcake.

new year's sparkler cupcakes

see variations page 149

Start the New Year with fireworks of your own. And don't worry; New Year's resolutions don't start until you wake up on New Year's Day, so you can still eat the cake!

cupcakes (page 16)
3 tbsp. buttercream per cupcake (page 19)
sparklers (indoors)

equipment
pencil, compasses, and scissors
black paper or black star cupcake wrappers
scotch tape

Frost the cupcakes using a Wilton 1M tip. Place the cupcakes into store-bought black star cupcake wrappers. Alternatively, you can make your own cupcake wrappers. Using a set of compasses, draw an arch at 2 1/4 in. and then the top arch at 4 in. onto the black paper. The arch should be at least 8 in. wide.

You can then add stars to the top by drawing around a 3/4-in. star cutter.

Cut the wrapper out and use as a template for other wrappers. Place the wrapper around the base of each cupcake and secure with a small piece of scotch tape.

When you are ready to serve, place the sparklers into the tops of the cupcakes and light.

Once the sparklers have gone out, carefully remove them. Be careful — they may still be very hot. It is advisable when using indoor sparklers to have a fire extinguisher on hand.

variations

valentine glittered heart cupcakes

see base recipe page 115

your-heart-in-my-heart cupcakes
Add a second, smaller heart to the center of the first heart. To provide contrast, don't glitter the second heart, or use a different color.

love heart cupcakes
Add the word "love" to a heart, either with an edible pen or using small alphabet craft stamps.

cupid's arrow cupcakes
Roll out black sugar paste to 1/10 in. thick and cut a strip 1/10 in. wide and 3/4 in. long. Add a black arrowhead and feathers to the tail. Attach to the heart using edible glue and allow to set for 12 hours before adding to a frosted cupcake.

brownie heart cupcakes
To create a delicious addition, use a heart cutter to cut out hearts from either store-bought or homemade dark brownies. Place on top of a cupcake that has been frosted with pink buttercream to set it off.

embossed heart cupcakes
To create a swirly design embossed heart, lightly grease an embossing mat with vegetable oil and wipe away any excess. Roll out the red sugar paste to 1/10 in. thick and lay on the embossing mat. Roll over the mat to imprint the sugar paste. Cut the heart from the embossed sugar paste and allow to dry for 12 hours before adding to frosted cupcakes.

variations

st. patrick's day cupcakes

see base recipe page 117

licorice shamrock cupcakes
Instead of using sugar paste for the shamrock, roll out some green sugared licorice and cut out the same heart shapes to give a frosted effect to the shamrock.

st. patrick's day leprechaun cupcakes
Create a leprechaun's hat by molding green sugar paste and adding an orange sugar-paste ribbon around its base. You can also add a small green shamrock to the ribbon. Allow to dry and add to the top of a frosted green buttercream cupcake.

st. patrick's day rainbow cupcakes
Place a rainbow-color strip of licorice into a green frosted cupcake to create a rainbow shape. At one end, place gold ball sprinkles or chocolate gold coins to denote the treasure at the end of the rainbow.

st. patrick's day irish flag cupcakes
Use green, white, and orange sugar paste rolled out to 1/4 in. thick, and create an Irish flag design by gluing the separate colored rectangles together. Allow to dry and place on top of a green frosted cupcake.

st. patrick's day cake
Place the green sugar-paste shamrocks around the side of a larger cake and place a large shamrock on the top. Finish with a green satin ribbon around the base of the cake.

variations

easter simnel cake

see base recipe page 118

mini simnel cakes
Create mini simnel cakes by baking the batter in muffin pans. After baking, cover the top with marzipan, add tiny apostle balls, and add a chick in eggshells.

marzipan lattice simnel cake
Create a lattice pattern with the strips of marzipan across the top of the simnel cake and add the apostle balls around the edge.

easter simnel cake with chocolate eggs
Instead of chicks, use chocolate-covered eggs as a central decoration.

chocolate simnel cake
Cover the top with chocolate sugar paste and add chocolate sugar-paste or malt balls for the apostles.

variations

spring bunny cupcakes

see base recipe page 121

cotton-tail bunny cupcake topper

Create a brown sugar-paste bunny bottom with a fluffy tail and place in a buttercream-grass cupcake.

daffodil cupcake topper

Use yellow sugar paste and a daffodil cutter to create a daffodil cupcake topper.

carrot cupcake topper

Use orange and green sugar paste to make carrot cupcake toppers.

easter bunny & carrot cake

Decorate a large cake with green buttercream grass-effect icing and decorate with a selection of bunny toppers and carrots.

easter basket cake

Use a Wilton no. 48 tip to create a basket weave around the side of a large round cake, create a grass effect on the top, and decorate with cupcake toppers.

variations

mother's day cupcakes

see base recipe page 122

picket fence cupcakes
Roll out white sugar paste to 1/4 in. thick and cut out 1/4-in.-wide rectangles with a peak end to create a picket fence, which you can place around the edge of the cupcake.

stripy cupcakes
Flat-ice the cupcake with alternating hot pink and pale pink sugar-paste stripes from the center of the cupcake outward.

mother's day bow cupcakes
Replace the rosebuds with a hot pink bow topper. Roll out the hot pink sugar paste to 1/10 in. thick and cut out 1/2-in.-wide stripes. Create the bow and support with paper towels between the loops until dry. Add a center ribbon and the tails.

rose tree cupcakes
Pipe green buttercream grass using a star tip to create the look of a topiary tree. Add small sugar-paste rolled roses and green leaves to the top of the cupcake.

rosebud mini cake
Decorate a mini cake with alternating hot pink and pale pink vertical stripes cascading from a central point on the top of the cake. Add 3 hot pink sugar-paste rosebuds and green leaves.

variations

ice-cream cone cupcakes

see base recipe page 125

ice cream cone with chocolate flake
Create a traditional ice-cream whip by adding a 2-in. chocolate flake into the frosting. Cut the flake in half lengthwise, otherwise it will be too heavy to sit upright.

strawberry sundae cake
Mold a strawberry out of red sugar paste and indent with a skewer to imitate the pits. Pour strawberry sauce around the frosted whip, then add an ice-cream wafer and the strawberry to the top.

brown derby sundae
Add a mini donut to the top of the cupcake, then add the frosted whip on top. Add chocolate sauce, sprinkles, and a cherry on top.

supersize sundae cake
Use the same technique to decorate a large cupcake cake to look like an ice-cream sundae, with multicolor sprinkles and a giant cherry on top.

root beer float cupcakes
Add sassafras or root beer extract to the cupcake batter before baking in brown cupcake wrappers. When cool, add the frosted whip and a cherry on top. Cut a drinking straw in half and push in to the whip.

variations

summer pinwheel cupcakes

see base recipe page 126

dotty pinwheel cupcakes
This technique works well with rolled-out sugar paste. Add contrasting spots on one side.

pastel pinwheel cupcakes
Use pastel toned sugar sheets to create the pinwheels, and place on top of cupcakes frosted with pastel-colored buttercream.

embossed summer pinwheel cupcakes
Emboss one side of the sugar paste and highlight with edible luster dust.

summer pinwheel cake
Make a large pinwheel to decorate the top of a fondant-covered square cake, and use edible glue to affix smaller pinwheels to the sides of the cake.

country pinwheel cupcakes
Use gingham sugar sheets to give a country garden feel to your pinwheels.

variations

star cupcakes

see base recipe page 128

star sprinkle cupcakes
Instead of making the gold stars, purchase edible gold star sprinkles for an equally shimmering effect.

new year toppers
Cut 2 1/4-in. circles from pale yellow sugar paste. Spray with edible gold luster spray. Allow to dry and add black year numbers using sugar-paste cutters or writing with a black edible pen. Place on top of a frosted cupcake.

new year's countdown toppers
Cut 2 1/4-in. circles from white sugar paste. Once dry, use a black edible pen to make the clock and add "12" at the top, with the two hands pointing up. Place on top of a frosted cupcake.

paper star cupcake toppers
Create golden-star paper cupcake toppers using gold paper, cutting out star shapes, and attaching a toothpick to the back of each one. You can also laminate the stars to ensure that they are food-safe and do not get soggy. Remove before eating.

variations

halloween cupcakes

see base recipe page 131

pumpkin cupcakes

Roll out orange sugar paste to 1/10 in. and cut out a pumpkin shape using a cutter or paper template. Allow to dry and add a range of scary faces with black edible pen.

witch's cat cupcakes

Roll out black sugar paste to 1/10 in. and cut out a cat silhouette using a cutter or paper template. Add neon or acid yellow sugar-paste eyes for a spooky effect.

ghost cupcakes

Roll out white sugar paste to 1/10 in. thick and cut out a ghost shape using a cutter or paper template. Allow to dry for 24 hours. Using a black edible pen, draw eyes and an "Oooo" mouth.

bat cupcakes

Roll out black sugar paste to 1/10 in. thick and cut out a bat shape using a cutter or paper template. Using a craft knife or blade tool, indent the veins of the bat wings. Add neon or acid yellow sugar-paste eyes for a spooky effect.

variations

nordic noel cake

see base recipe page 132

nordic bauble cupcakes and cake pops
Use the bauble decorating technique to decorate cupcakes and cake pops.

nordic noel bauble cake
Cover a 6-inch cake with sugar paste and decorate to look like one large bauble.

christmas stocking cake
Instead of baubles, cut out Christmas stockings and hang them around the edge of the cake. Pipe family members' names on the stockings.

bauble wreath cake
Make the baubles slightly rounded and arrange on top of the cake to look like a bauble wreath.

nordic noel cookies
Use the same piping technique to decorate a cookie covered in sugar paste.

variations

christmas tree cupcakes

see base recipe page 135

giant christmas tree cupcake
Transfer the Christmas tree design to a giant cupcake cake. Cover the base with red sugar paste and pipe the green buttercream on the top. Create large baubles by cutting 3/4-in. circles from colored sugar paste and top off with a yellow sugar-paste star.

christmas tree cupcake tier
Arrange the cupcakes on a tiered cake stand and only place a large yellow sugar-paste star on the top cupcake.

douglas fir cupcake
To create a different piping effect, use a star tip instead of the 1M tip. Pipe fir branches from the center outward, layering this effect until the tip of the tree. Decorate in the same way.

multicolor christmas tree cupcakes
To create a different 2-tone color effect, add 2 shades of green to the piping bag before piping.

tinselled christmas tree cupcakes
Using a PME no. 2 tip, pipe red swags around the Christmas tree to imitate tinsel.

variations

new year's sparkler cupcakes

see base recipe page 136

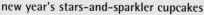

new year's stars-and-sparkler cupcakes

Add sugar-paste stars sprayed with either gold or silver luster spray.

new year's number sparkler cupcakes

Using a 2-in. round cutter, make a sugar-paste circle and pipe or use a black edible pen to write the new year number. Place on the cupcake topper sitting up so you can still add the sparkler behind.

champagne celebration cupcakes

Using bottle green sugar paste, mold a champagne bottle with a sugar-paste brown cork. Add a white sugar-paste label and paint with gold luster paint. Serve the cupcake in a saucer-style champagne glass for a festive display.

curlicue cupcakes

Curl 1/4-in.-wide strips of colored sugar paste around a pencil. Allow to dry and remove carefully. Add to the top of a frosted cupcake and sprinkle with confetti sprinkles.

graduation cupcakes

Use a 2-in. round cutter to make a sugar-paste circle and pipe or use a black edible pen to write "class of XXXX." Place on the cupcake topper sitting up so you can still add the sparkler behind.

embellishments

Whether you'd like to update a classic, or try a new

skill, this chapter has plenty of projects to take you

to the next level!

damask flower cake

see variations page 171

Sugar sheets aren't just for photo cakes. They come in a range of sumptuous designs.

2-layer cake covered in white sugar paste
(pages 12, 20)
sugar paste in white and black
Wilton damask sugar sheet

equipment
pencil, ruler, scissors, and paper
2-in. daisy cutter
1 1/4-in. daisy cutter
flower forming cup

Unwrap the sugar sheet. We used a black-and-white damask design sheet. Calculate the length of the border on both layers of the cake and calculate the available width, allowing for 7 petals also to be cut from the sheet. We used a 1-inch-wide border. Mark the back of the sheet with a pencil and ruler, and cut the borders carefully using scissors. Attach to the base of each layer of the cake with water.

Create a paper petal template at least 3 1/4 in. long and copy 7 petals onto the back of the remaining sugar sheet. Cut out the petals carefully. Using an edible black pen, create a 1/10-in. border around each petal. Roll out the black sugar paste to 1/10 in. thick. Using the 2-in. and 1 1/4-in. daisy cutters, cut out 2 daisies and glue together to form the center of the flower. Glue a white sugar-paste center ball 1/2 in. wide.

Place a small ball of white sugar paste on the center of a flower forming cup and arrange the petals and glue in place. Glue the black daisy center in the middle. Allow to dry for 24 hours. Add the flower offset to the base of the second tier of the cake. Glue a small ball of white sugar paste to the cake, and then attach the flower with glue to this ball. The sugar paste will allow you to position the flower to the desired angle.

cameo brooch cupcakes

see variations page 172

Pretty as a picture, these beautiful brooches will amaze and delight. If you can't find gold dragées, roll tiny balls of sugar paste and cover with gold edible paint.

cupcakes baked in cream liners (page 16)
3 tbsp. buttercream per cupcake (page 19)
vegetable oil
sugar paste in white, coral and gold
gold edible dragées (optional)
gold edible paint

equipment
brooch mold
paintbrush

Lightly spray or rub vegetable oil over the mold to prevent sticking. Wipe away any excess. Place the coral sugar paste in the stone part of the mold and gently press into place. Add gold dragées, if desired. Gently place the gold sugar paste over the rest of the mold and press into place. Remove any excess from the back of the mold before turning out the brooch. Roll out some white sugar paste, cut out a silhouette, and place on the center of the stone.

Repeat the process for each cupcake. Allow to dry for 12 hours. Paint the gold parts of the brooch with edible paint. Allow to dry and then place on frosted cupcakes.

lace dress embossed cupcakes

see variations page 173

These elegant toppers are a great project on which to learn how to use embossing mats. Make sure the mat is coated lightly and evenly with vegetable oil before starting — low-calorie sprays are perfect for this, and less messy than rubbing oil on with a paper towel.

cupcakes baked in black liners (page 16)
1/2 quantity buttercream (page 19)
vegetable oil
sugar paste in white and black
white alcohol
black food coloring paste

equipment
texture mat
dress template
paintbrush

Lightly spray or rub vegetable oil over the texture mat and remove any excess with a paper towel. This will prevent the mat from sticking to the sugar paste. Roll out the white sugar paste to 1/10 in. and place the texture mat over the sugar paste. Firmly roll over the mat to create the patterned sugar paste.

Use a template to cut out a dress shape with a craft knife. Use a mixture of white alcohol and black food coloring paste to create an edible paint, and lightly paint over the raised pattern. Roll out the black sugar paste to 1/8 in. thick and use a craft knife to cut strips for the waistband and the sash. Fix in place with edible glue or water.

Repeat the process for each cupcake. Allow to dry overnight and place on frosted cupcakes.

button cake

see variations page 173

You can make the buttons for this project weeks in advance; simply dry them and store in an airtight container. Then it won't take long to assemble the cake when you're ready!

prepared 6-in. and 8-in. 2-layer cake covered
    with peach sugar paste (pages 12, 20)
sugar paste in white, blue, red, orange, purple,
    and green
pearlized luster spray

equipment
selection of small circle and other shape cutters
metal piping tube
serrated cone tool

Mix a range of pastel-colored sugar pastes, including pale blue, pink, peach, lilac, and green, to create the buttons. Roll out the different colors of sugar paste to 1/4 in. thick and, using a selection of small cutters to create a range of button shapes, cut out some of the following examples from each color:

• 1/2-in. circle: indent the center with the end of a craft knife and add 2 or 4 buttonholes with the end of a skewer.

• Using the craft knife, cut out 3/4-in. squares, indent with the end of a piping tube, and add 2 buttonholes with a skewer.

• Cut 2 1/4-in. circles and mark the edge with the side of a serrated cone tool or toothpick. Add buttonholes with a skewer.

• Create heart shapes and diamonds using the same technique.

• Roll small balls of white sugar paste 1/2 in. across and press gently with your finger. Add 4 buttonholes and spray with pearlized luster spray to create pearl buttons.

You will need about 150 buttons in a mix of sizes, shapes, and colors. After 15 minutes of drying time, the buttons will be ready to glue on the side of the cake. Try to create a pattern with the buttons before gluing to ensure the colors and designs are mixed. Glue the buttons to both layers of the cake, starting from the bottom and working up to three quarters of the way up each layer, or until your buttons run out.

victoria sponge cake

see variations page 175

This is a pretty way to update the classic tea party favorite.

two 8-in. sponge cakes, sandwiched together
with strawberry jam and 10 tbsp.
buttercream, with a further 10 tbsp.
buttercream piped on top (pages 12, 19, 20)
sugar paste in pale blue, green, red, and white
red edible pen

equipment
serrated kitchen knife
2-in. scalloped-edge round cutter
1/2-in. daisy plunger cutter
cone tool
2 1/4-in. rose leaf plunger cutter
1/2-in. blossom flower plunger cutter

Roll out the pale blue sugar paste to 1/4 in. thick and cut out nine 2-in. scalloped-edge circles. Roll out the green sugar paste to 1/10 in. thick and cut out 9 strawberry husks using a 1/2-in. daisy plunger cutter. Mold 9 thin strawberry stalks to match.

Mold nine 3/4-in.-long strawberries from the red sugar paste and prick with a toothpick to resemble the pits. Indent the top of each strawberry with a cone tool and insert the green husk, securing with glue. Then glue in a green stalk. From the same green sugar paste, cut out 8 rose leaves using the plunger leaf cutter. Roll out the white sugar paste to 1/10 in. thick and cut out 18 blossoms. Use the red edible pen to dot the centers of the blossoms.

Glue the leaf, strawberry, and 2 blossoms to each blue disc and place the discs evenly around the edge of the cake, with one in the center.

russian doll cake

see variations page 176

The trees and flowers can be fiddly to stick on once dried, and are best left to dry on the cake. Allow at least 24 hours for this.

rectangle cake covered with blue sugar paste
    (pages 12, 20)
sugar paste in pale pink, red, pale peach, brown,
    white, blue, and green

equipment
russian doll–shape paper templates in different
    sizes
selection of circle cutters for the faces
scalloped circle cutter

Make paper templates of the dolls and make sure they fit nicely onto your cake. Roll out the pale pink sugar paste and use the templates to cut out 8 doll shapes varying in size. Roll out the red sugar paste and lay the first doll on top. Cut around the doll's head for the scarf. Remove the doll and cut away where the scarf would end. Repeat for all the dolls.

Roll out the pale peach sugar paste and cut out 8 faces with circle cutters, varying the sizes accordingly. Glue each face to the pink dolls.

Use the same circle cutters to cut brown sugar-paste circles for the hair. Cut away 2 pieces and glue to the face. Cut a face hole in each of the red sugar-paste hoods, making sure you use the same cutter for the doll's hood and face. Glue the hood in place.

Roll out the white sugar paste, cut an apron for each doll, and glue in place. Roll out the blue sugar paste and cut a large scalloped circle. Cut along just inside the scallop and arrange the scalloped edge around the apron.

Cut red sugar-paste flowers for the apron and scarf, and glue in place. Use a circle cutter to cut small leaves from green sugar paste to decorate the apron, and then glue in lace from white sugar paste. Use the same technique to cut ends for the scarves, and add eyes and mouth. Mold trees from brown sugar paste and glue to the cake with cutout flowers.

Use the heart cutter together with green sugar-paste leaves to make a pattern on the sides of the cake. Finish the bottom of the cake with more cutout leaves. Let dry for 24 hours.

circle cake

see variations page 177

It can be tricky to get the stripes level; lightly mark guide points at the appropriate heights for each with a ruler before you start.

2-layer cake covered with white sugar paste
(pages 12, 20)
sugar paste in blue, red, and green

equipment
circle cutter, about half the depth of your cake
greaseproof paper and pencil

Start by drawing around your circle cutter on greaseproof paper. Draw a line vertically and horizontally through the circle so it's divided into quarters. Use this as a guide for all of your circles. Roll out the blue sugar paste to 1/10 in. thick and cut out a circle. Place the circle on your guide. Use the cutter to cut away 2 sections by placing your cutter so that a quarter of it intersects the sugar-paste circle at 9 o'clock to 12 o'clock, and then at 12 o'clock to 3 o'clock. Glue with the bottom of the circle along the base of the cake.

Roll out the red sugar paste, cut a circle, and place on the guide. Cut away at each quarter with the circle cutter. Keep 2 of the cutouts to one side and glue the bottom 2 cutouts on the cake to complete the blue circle.

Roll out the green sugar paste, cut a circle, and place on the guide. Cut away the 4 quarters using the circle cutter. Affix the remaining star shape to the cake and affix the remaining two red cutouts to complete the circle. Repeat the blue circle again and affix the opposite way. Continue the pattern around until you have covered the cake. For the top layer, roll out the sugar paste to 1/10 in. thick. Cut strips long enough to go all the way around the cake and glue into position.

silhouette plaque cake

see variations page 178

If you have a profile photo of the cake's recipient, trace it for your silhouette.

8-in. square cake covered with white sugar paste
(pages 12, 20)
sugar paste in pale pink, black, and white

equipment
set of compasses or 7-in.-diameter plate
paper, pen, and scissors
blade tool
1-in.-wide satin ribbon

Use a compass or draw around a 7-inch-diameter plate on paper to create the circle template. Cut it out with the scissors. Roll out the pale pink sugar paste to 1/4 in. thick and cut out the circle. Carefully place in the center of the top of the cake and smooth flat.

Take the circle template and design your silhouette within, ensuring there is at least a 3/4-in. border clear around the edge. Try to keep it simple. Cut out the template. Roll out the black sugar paste to 1/4 in. thick and cut around the silhouette template using a craft knife. Tidy up the edges with a blade tool and smooth the surface with a cake smoother or your hand.

Add some of the edible glue to the surface of the pink circle and place the face silhouette on top. Smooth again. Using black, pale pink, and white sugar paste, create 1/4-in. balls and glue around the edge of the plaque. You will need about 30 of each color.

To create the frill ribbon effect around the base, roll out the pale pink sugar paste to 1/10 in. thick and cut 1 1/4-in.-wide strips. Fan 1 edge by squeezing between your fingers. Glue the strips around the base of the cake with the fanned edge down. Cover the top of the frill with a satin ribbon, secured at the back with a pin.

chocolate malt balls cake

see variations page 179

You could also tie a ribbon around the middle of the cake and secure at the front with a bow. Not only will this look pretty, but it will also provide support for the ladyfingers.

two 8-in. round chocolate sponge cakes (page 15)
14 oz. chocolate buttercream (page 19)
2 boxes of chocolate-covered ladyfingers
10 oz. chocolate malt balls

equipment
silver floral wire (24-gauge)

Sandwich the 2 cakes together with a third of the chocolate buttercream. Place the bottom of the sponge facing up to ensure a flat surface. Check that a vertical chocolate ladyfinger fits the side of the cake and exceeds the top by 3/4 in. If it's short, you can add a ring of malt balls around the base. Cover the sides of the cake with chocolate buttercream and immediately place the chocolate ladyfingers vertically around the side.

Cover the top of the cake with the remaining buttercream and immediately place the chocolate malt balls on top in a neat circular pattern. Leave the center free, about the size of 1 malt ball.

Cut 8-inch lengths of the wire and curl around a wooden spoon to create a curlicue effect. Insert a chocolate malt ball into the top of the wire. You will need at least 7 wires. Insert the wires into the center of the cake.

falling star cake

see variations page 180

Before cutting out the stars, decide the order in which your colored stars will fall. Try looking at a color wheel to see which colors work best next to each other.

2-layer cake covered with white sugar paste
(pages 12, 20)
selection of sugar-paste colors

equipment
different-size star cutters
ribbon (optional)

Roll out all the sugar-paste colors and cut out a selection of different-size stars. Starting at the top of the cake, begin to fix the stars in place with edible glue or a small ball of soft sugar paste.

Change the colors of the stars as you work down and across the front of the cake. Continue to add stars until you reach the bottom of the cake.

If you're not happy with the bottom finish of your cake, attach a ribbon to the bottom of the cakes before you add the stars.

bunting cake

see variations page 181

Make a celebration special with these decorative flags.

prepared 8-in. sponge cake covered with white
    sugar paste (pages 12, 20)
6-in. square polka-dot sugar sheet
sugar paste in white, red, and green
red and green edible paint

equipment
thin-tip paintbrush
scissors
1 1/4-in. heart cutter
red polka-dot 1 1/4-in.-wide satin ribbon

Roll out the white sugar paste to 1/4 in. thick and cut out 12 triangle flags, 4 x 5.2-in. each.
Allow to dry for 24 hours. Using red and green edible paint, paint 8 of the flags with a
selection of small rosebuds with green leaves. Using scissors, cut out another 6 flags from
the polka-dot sugar sheet, the same size as the others. Use a 1 1/4-in. heart cutter and
simply press out 6 hearts from the polka-dot sugar sheet and attach to the center of 6 of
the white flags with water. Glue the bunting to the side of the cake in groups of 5 in a
regular sweeping pattern.

Roll the red sugar paste into thin, 1/10-in.-wide sausages to create the bunting ribbon. Glue
to the top of the bunting and attach the rosebuds and leaves at the join. Finish with a polka-
dot satin ribbon secured around the base.

damask flower cake

see base recipe page 151

damask stripe cake
Use the sugar sheet to create vertical stripes on the first layer of the cake. Simply measure with a ruler and carefully cut with scissors. Apply to the cake using a brush and a small amount of water.

damask cake with daisies
Instead of using the large flower to decorate, roll out black sugar paste to 1/10 in. thick and cut out small daisies. Cut small 1/2-in. circles or use a small circle cutter from the sugar sheet, and glue to the centers of the flowers. Decorate all over both layers of the cake.

all-over damask flowers
Cut out the individual patterns from the damask pattern and attach around the sides of a single-layer cake to create a more silhouette look.

damask cupcakes
Cut out circles from the sugar sheet using a 2 1/2-in. round cutter and add to the tops of cupcakes that have had a light skim of buttercream to create coordinating cupcakes.

co-ordinating flower cupcakes
Create smaller flowers to place on cupcakes. Create a smaller petal template and copy 7 petals onto the back of the sugar sheet. Cut and arrange into a flower mold and allow to dry. Place on the top of a frosted cupcake with a white sugar-paste ball center.

cameo brooch cupcake

see base recipe page 153

opal brooch cupcake
Use 2 tones of blue color to look like a turquoise stone when making the precious stone of the brooch. Omit the silhouette.

brooch cake
Make a large brooch, and use to decorate a multiple-layer cake.

pearl cameo brooch cupcake
In place of the pink brooch center, mix a very small amount of teddy-bear brown sugar paste with white sugar paste, and paint with cream luster dust to create a pearl effect.

rosette brooch cupcake
Cut sugar-paste strips and pleat into a rosette. Place brooch in the center and use to decorate cakes or cupcakes.

variations

lace dress embossed cupcakes

see base recipe page 154

3-d embossed dress cupcakes
Hand-pipe the detail of the embossed dress with royal icing to give a 3-D effect, and add a sugar-paste blossom flower to the waistband.

wedding dress cupcakes
Roll out some white sugar paste to 1/10 in. thick and cut out a dress bodice shape. Add edible pearl sprinkles to the neck of the bodice with glue. Allow to dry for 12 hours. After baking, turn the cupcake upside down and cover with a thin layer of buttercream. Then cover with a large circle of white fondant, adding ruffles to the skirt as you lay it. Place the bodice into the top of the skirt and spray the whole cupcake with pearl luster spray.

ruffle ballerina cupcakes
As per the original recipe, create a dress bodice using pale pink sugar paste. Allow to dry for 12 hours. Bake cupcakes in pale pink liners and, using pale pink frosting, pipe 3 layers of ruffles with a Wilton no. 104 petal tip to form the ballerina skirt. Add the bodice to the top.

princess cake
Create a large cake skirt using a dome-shaped tin. Cover the cake with pink buttercream ruffles and add a cake doll to the top with a sugar-paste crown.

variations

button cake

see base recipe page 156

button cupcakes
Place a range of similar buttons on top of frosted cupcakes baked in complementing pastel cupcake liners.

new baby button cupcakes
Create new baby or baby shower cupcakes by flat-icing a cupcake with sugar paste and placing a single button in the middle. Write "Cute as a button" with edible pen around the button.

christmas button cake
Use a selection of red sugar-paste buttons in different shapes to create a Christmas tree shape on top of a square cake. Finish with a festive ribbon around the base.

valentine's button cake
Make a selection of red and pink sugar-paste buttons, including heart shapes, and form a heart shape on top of a heart-shaped cake for Valentine's Day.

butterfly button cake
Create a butterfly-shaped cake and cover with butterfly-shaped buttons. Use a 1-inch butterfly cutter and a skewer to imprint the buttonholes.

variations

victoria sponge cake

see base recipe page 159

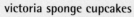

victoria sponge cupcakes
Create complementary cupcakes by placing the strawberry discs on top of frosted cupcakes.

victoria sponge cake with fresh strawberries
Use fresh strawberries in the filling and as a decoration on top.

victoria sponge valentine's cupcakes
Cut a fresh strawberry vertically to create a heart shape and add to the top of cupcakes frosted with chocolate buttercream. Ideal for Valentine's cupcakes.

victoria sponge butterfly cakes
Use a serrated knife to slice off the top of baked victoria sponge cupcakes, keeping the slices to one side. Using a spoon, scoop out the centers of the cupcakes and discard. Fill with buttercream and strawberry jam. Cut the cupcake top slices in half vertically, invert, and place on top of the buttercream and jam, to resemble butterfly wings. Sprinkle with confectioners' sugar.

raspberry and chocolate cake
Replace the victoria sponge with chocolate sponge, and the buttercream with chocolate buttercream. Replace the strawberry preserves with raspberry preserves, and shape small raspberries in place of the sugar-paste strawberries.

variations

russian doll cake

see base recipe page 161

doll cake
Use a sheet-baked sponge cake and cut around a large doll template before covering with sugar paste and decorating in the same way.

name russian doll cake
Add names to the dolls' aprons so each guest has a slice with her name on it.

russian doll cookies
Use the same decorating technique to make sugar paste–covered cookies for party favors.

owl cake
This design also works well when the dolls are substituted with a family of owls.

variations

circle cake

see base recipe page 163

red and white circle cake
For a more basic version, use only the red sections on a white cake and continue the pattern so that the circles intertwine.

simple circle cake
Create a similar effect by simplifying the design. Place each full circle next to each other rather than overlapping the design.

ring cake
An alternative design would be to cut out a circle and cut away a smaller circle off center. Randomly place these over the cake.

circle cupcakes
Make coordinating cupcakes with circle toppers on frosted cupcakes and flat-iced cupcakes with stripes.

variations

silhouette plaque cake

see base recipe page 164

silhouette plaque cupcakes
Create complementing cupcake toppers, but use scalloped-edge circle cutters to make the plaque and cut smaller silhouettes and glue to the plaques. Allow to dry and place on top of frosted cupcakes.

silhouette plaque multilayer cake
Create an oval plaque that could be placed on the front of a multilayer round cake. Place satin ribbon around the middle of the cake and add the plaque on top.

bon voyage cake
Add a cityscape silhouette on top of the cake, in place of the portrait silhouette.

halloween silhouette plaque cake
Create a haunted Halloween house silhouette that can be placed on top of a square cake covered in orange sugar paste. Use neon sugar paste for the windows and add a few spooky silhouettes in the windows.

silhouette baby shower cake
Create a personalized baby shower cake by adding a silhouette of the pregnant mom-to-be with a pink heart on her stomach.

variations

chocolate malt balls cake

see base recipe page 167

white chocolate malt balls cake
Use white chocolate-covered ladyfingers and white chocolate malt balls for a more feminine effect. You could also add a pink ribbon and a bow.

malt balls cupcakes
Use the malt balls as cupcake toppers.

chocolate finger cake
Use chocolate Kit Kat fingers around the side of the cake instead of malt balls.

rocky road cake
Create a Rocky Road–decorated cake with a mix of malt balls and marshmallows drizzled with melted chocolate.

black-and-white malt balls cake
Create a patterned malt-ball cake by alternating the design of milk chocolate and white chocolate malt balls, covering the entire cake.

chocolate malt balls ice cream cake
Split the cake and fill with vanilla or chocolate ice cream. Freeze for at least 30 minutes before decorating as main project. Serve immediately.

variations

falling star cake

see base recipe page 168

falling flower cake
Use flowers in place of the stars for a more feminine-feel birthday.

number star cake
Add sugar-paste numbers to the larger stars to celebrate a particular age birthday.

falling snowflake cake
Use white snowflakes in place of the stars for a beautiful Christmas cake finish, with a metallic ribbon around the base of each tier.

falling star cupcakes
Use the star cutouts to decorate cupcakes or sugar paste-covered cookies for party favors.

star spray cake
Insert wires into the stars and arrange in the top of the cake.

fall cake
Use leaf cutters to make fall-colored leaves, and glue on in random patterns.

meteor shower cake
Cut white stars, and use on top of a cake covered in dark-blue sugar paste.

variations

bunting cake

see base recipe page 170

bunting cupcakes
Use the same designs of flags to create bunting cupcakes. Use a smaller bunting size so that 3 flags can fit on each cupcake. Flat-ice the cupcake and glue the flags in place.

bunting birthday cake
Use brightly colored bunting flags for a child's birthday, and add the child's age to the center flag using a number cutter or an edible pen.

bunting cake with paper bunting topper
Create a paper bunting cake topper: cut diamond shapes from colorful paper and fold over a string or ribbon and glue together. Repeat until enough flags cover the width of string to match the width of the cake. Attach each end of the bunting to 2 skewers and insert each skewer into the top of the cake, allowing the bunting to sweep over the top of the cake.

national flag bunting cake
Create bunting to incorporate your national or state flag for official celebrations. Cut out the bunting in white sugar paste and allow to dry for 24 hours before painting the flag design in edible pen colors.

bunting name cake
Make larger bunting flags to place on the top of the cake, and pipe or write a letter from the recipient's name on each flag.

flowers

Elegant, refined, and yet completely delicious,

sugarcraft flowers add a touch of glamour to any

cake. This chapter presents a wide range of

romantic, pretty decorations to choose from.

primrose teapot cake

see variations page 203

Make the handle and spout as delicate as possible; too heavy and they won't stick.

8-in. cake covered with white sugar paste
(pages 12, 20)
white sugar paste
edible cocoa butter
gold, yellow, and green edible luster dust

equipment
4-in. polystyrene craft ball
cocktail stick
paintbrush
greaseproof paper and pencil

Start by rolling out the white sugar paste to 1/10 in. thick and cover the polystyrene ball. Use the white sugar paste to mold a handle, spout, and lid. When you are happy with the shape, insert a cocktail stick about halfway into the end of the spout. It needs to be able to support the weight of the spout once inserted into the cake. Repeat this for the handle. Allow to dry for 24 hours. Assemble your teapot, securing with edible glue.

Place some of the cocoa butter on a saucer resting over a cup of warm water; this helps keep the butter at a good working temperature. You can use this saucer as your palette. Use edible luster dust or food coloring paste mixed with the cocoa butter to create edible paint.

You can paint freehand onto your teapot or trace a picture of primroses onto some greaseproof paper. Invert the image by drawing over it on the reverse side and trace the outline onto the teapot. Once painted, allow to dry before affixing in place on top of your cake.

rose posy cake

see variations page 204

Soft, romantic roses suit any occasion.

8-in. sponge cake covered in pale blue
  sugar paste (pags 12, 20)
sugar paste in red, purple, and white

equipment
2 1/2-in. 5-petal rose cutter
ball tool
sponge or foam mat

Create 3 shades of dusty pink sugar paste, by adding red and a little purple sugar paste to white sugar paste. Then add this to more white sugar paste to create 2 paler shades. Create the center bud of the rose in the main dusty pink shade by molding a 2-in.-tall bottle shape. Flatten the neck of the bottle and then pinch the top together.

Roll out the main dusty pink shade to 1/10 in. thick and use a 2 1/2-in. 5-petal rose cutter. Fan the tips of each petal with your finger or a ball tool on a sponge or foam mat. Glue each petal around the center bud, but before you seal it in place, add the next petal. When you have secured all 5 petals, trim any excess sugar paste from the base and allow to dry for at least an hour.

Roll out the next shade of pink sugar paste to 1/10 in. and repeat the process of cutting, fanning, and gluing the petals in place. Once you have added 5 petals, allow to dry for another hour. Roll out the final shade of pink sugar paste and use the same technique to add the outer petals. You may need as many as 7 petals to complete the flower. Curl the ends of these petals over with your finger to create a realistic effect. Repeat the process to create a second rose. Allow the roses to dry for at least 24 hours before adding to the top of the cake with edible glue.

moth orchid cake

see variations page 205

Available from specialty suppliers, flower paste dries quicker and harder than sugar paste
and you can roll it much more thinly than sugar paste to create delicate flowers.

4-in. cake covered with white sugar paste,
    (pages 12, 20)
flower paste in white, yellow, and green
yellow food coloring paste
pink food coloring paste
clear alcohol

equipment
moth orchid cutters and veiners
forming cup
shaping foam mat
ball tool

Roll out the white flower paste to 1/10 in. thick and use the 3-leaf moth orchid cutter for
the back leaves. Press gently between the veiner and put in a forming cup. Cut 2 single
round leaves. Press between the veiner and place in the forming cup over the existing leaf.
Use a little edible glue to secure in place.

Cut the labellum from the white flower paste and place on the foam mat. Cut the bottom
triangle in half. Use a ball tool to gently curl the top, 2 sides, and bottom so that the
labellum has curled up. Roll a small ball of yellow flower paste. Press into a sausage shape
and flatten, indent through the middle, and glue to the center of the labellum. Fix the
labellum to the petals in the forming cup and allow to dry.

Mix some yellow food coloring paste with clear alcohol and paint the center of the moth
orchid. Using the same method, paint pink onto the orchid and allow to dry. Use the green
sugar paste to make a stem and glue in place on the cake. Arrange the orchids on the cake
and glue in place.

blossom cupcakes

see variations page 206

Celebrate spring with a spray of beautiful blossoms.

cupcakes baked in white liners (page 16)
3 tbsp. buttercream per cupcake (page 19)
sugar paste in orange, pink, and white

equipment
1/4-in. blossom plunger cutter
shaping foam mat
piping bag
Wilton 1M tip

Create peach sugar paste by adding a small amount of orange and pink sugar paste to white sugar paste. Create a paler shade of peach by adding this main shade to white sugar paste. Repeat to create a third, very pale peach shade.

Roll out one of the sugar-paste colors to 1/10 in. thick. Cut the flower from the sugar paste using the plunger cutter and push it out onto the shaping foam mat. As you push the plunger into the mat, the petals will curl up. Repeat this step for all 3 colors until you have enough flowers to cover the cupcake, about 30 blossoms.

Repeat the process for each cupcake. Allow the blossoms to dry. Pipe a buttercream swirl over each cupcake and work quickly to stick a mixture of colored blossoms to the buttercream.

tropical flowers cake

see variations page 207

Perfect for a luau or a summer birthday, these flowers are simply stunning.

2-layer cake covered with blue sugar paste
white flower paste (pages 12, 20, 23)
yellow edible luster dust or food coloring gel
clear alcohol
pale gold sugar paste
4 graham crackers, crushed

equipment
2 1/4-in. five-petal cutter
shaping foam mat
ball tool
forming cup
blade tool

Start by rolling out the white flower paste and cutting out a flower shape with the petal cutter. Using the craft knife, cut along the edges of each petal to the center so you have 5 single petals. Place each petal in turn on the foam mat and use the ball tool to curl up the edges of the petals. Arrange the petals in a forming cup so that each petal has one side overlapping the next petal, resembling a tropical flower. Glue in place. Allow the flowers to dry overnight and paint the centers with a mixture of yellow luster dust and clear alcohol.

For the auger shell, roll some pale gold sugar paste into a cone shape and use the blade tool to gently press and roll the shell in one movement to add an indent. For the clamshell, mold the shell shape and use the ball tool to curve the shell underneath and the blade tool to add ridges on top.

When the shells are dry, arrange around the base of the cake and add crushed graham crackers to create sand. Use the shell technique to create some starfish. Carefully glue the tropical flowers around the first layer and on top of the cake.

summer vintage rose cupcakes

see variations page 208

Hand-painting is a wonderful way to get creative. For an even distribution of flowers, gently mark the centers of the flowers with the end of the paintbrush.

cupcakes baked in hot pink liners
   (page 16)
1 tbsp. buttercream per cupcake (page 19)
blue sugar paste
pink and green edible luster dust
clear alcohol

equipment
2 1/2-in. round cutter
paintbrush

Roll out the blue sugar paste to 1/4 in. thick and cut out a circle with the 2 1/2-in. round cutter. Add a tablespoon of buttercream to the top of the cupcake and lay the blue disc on top. Smooth flat with the palm of your hand.

Mix the edible luster dust and clear alcohol together to make edible pink paint and green paint. You only need a small amount of alcohol to get the right consistency. Using the pink paint, make small circular swirl markings to create a rose. You don't need too much detail, just the rough shape of a rose. Repeat, spacing out your roses across your cupcake. Use the green paint to add leaves to each of the roses.

Repeat the process for each cupcake. Allow to dry before serving.

hand-piped rose cupcakes

see variations page 209

Practice makes perfect when learning to pipe these roses, but they're easy once you get the hang of them!

cupcakes baked in silver or yellow liners
    (page 16)
3 tbsp. yellow buttercream per cupcake
    (page 19)
green sugar paste

equipment
1/2-in rose leaf cutter
piping bag
Wilton no. 104 petal tip

Roll out the green sugar paste and cut out a rose leaf with the 1/2-in rose leaf cutter. Allow to dry for an hour or so.

Fill the piping bag with buttercream and attach a Wilton no. 104 petal tip. Position the tip on the center of the cupcake with the wide end of the tip touching the cake and the thin point at the top. Apply pressure and turn the cupcake a full turn until you have piped a cone shape. Repeat this movement for the first leaf, rotating around a third of the cupcake.

Use the same process for the second leaf, but start a third back from the end of the first leaf so that the petals overlap. Continue this method until the cupcake is full.

Insert the leaf while the rose is still wet.

vanity rose cake

see variations page 210

This rose needs to dry for as long as possible — at least 24 hours. It will dry on the outside long before the center is ready to be lifted, so take extra care when transferring to the cake.

6-in. cake covered with white sugar paste
   (pages 12, 20)
pink flower paste
edible pearl dragées

equipment
5-petal flower cutters in 3 sizes
foam mat
ball tool
forming cup
pink satin ribbon

Roll out the pink flower paste to 1/8 in. and cut out a flower using the largest flower cutter. Gently place the flower on the foam mat, and use a ball tool to thin the petal edges and curl them inward. Place the flower in a forming cup to dry. Repeat this process with the same size cutter and glue on top of the first flower, but rotated so that the petals cover the gaps in the petals below.

Make the next 2 flowers using the middle cutter, and continue to rotate the flowers as you affix them to the bloom. Make the next 2 flowers using the smallest cutter and affix to the center of the bloom.

Glue some pearl dragées to the center of the bloom and allow to dry for at least 24 hours before placing on top of the mini cake. Place a pink satin ribbon around the base of the cake and secure at the back with a pin.

quilted flower cupcakes

see variations page 211

Practice indenting the lines before working on the real thing; it's important to have consistent pressure along the whole line.

cupcakes baked in cream liners (page 16)
1 tbsp. buttercream per cupcake (page 19)
sugar paste in light brown and white
edible pearl dragées

equipment
2-in. 5-petal rose cutter
blade tool
2 1/2-in. round cutter

Mix cream sugar paste by adding a small amount of light brown to white sugar paste. Roll out the cream sugar paste to 1/4 in. thick and, using a craft knife, cut a 1 1/4 x 1/2-in. rectangle. Smooth the top edge with your finger. Starting at one end, roll the sugar paste between your two fingers, pinching at the base, forming the rosebud center. Using a 2-in. rose cutter, cut out 5 petal shapes. Add each petal to the rosebud, crossing over the last petal to form a small rose. Cut any excess off the base.

To create the quilted cupcake covering, roll out the cream sugar paste to 1/4 in. thick. Using a blade tool or craft knife, indent lines 1/2 in. apart and then repeat with adjacent lines. Use a 2 1/2-in. round cutter to cut a disc from the quilted sugar paste. Spoon a tablespoon of buttercream onto the top of the cupcake. Place the quilted disk over the buttercream to cover the cupcake. Be careful not to smooth away the imprint.

Glue pearl dragées at the quilt joins. Attach the rose, offset to the center of the top of the cupcake. Secure with edible glue, if needed. Repeat the process for each cupcake.

hydrangea cake & cupcake tower

see variations page 212

If you'd like the whole cake to be edible, you could carve a hemisphere from a smaller cake in place of the polystyrene ball. Cover with white sugar paste and proceed as directed.

cake covered with white sugar paste (pages 12, 20)
pale blue sugar paste
blue edible luster dust
edible pearl dragées

equipment
hydrangea cutter and veiner
paintbrush
half of 4-in. polystyrene ball

Roll out the pale blue sugar paste to 1/10 in. thick and cut out 3 hydrangea flowers using the hydrangea cutter. Place each flower on the veiner and gently press together. Use the luster dust and paintbrush to dust a darker center on each hydrangea flower. Glue a pearl dragée to the center of each flower. Arrange the 3 flowers together so that they are folded up and supporting each other. Allow to dry in this position.

Repeat this process until you have enough flowers to cover the half polystyrene ball and the cupcakes. Allow to dry.

Cover the half polystyrene ball with rolled-out sugar paste and use edible glue to affix the hydrangea flowers in place over the ball. Use a little sugar-paste ball to hold the flowers, if needed. Use the remaining flowers to cover frosted cupcakes.

vintage rosebud cupcakes

see variations page 213

These little rosebuds are just adorable, and they're so easy to make that they are a perfect choice for decorating a large number of cupcakes.

cupcakes baked in silver liners (page 16)
1 tbsp. buttercream per cupcake (page 19)
sugar paste in white, green, and red

equipment
small leaf cutter or plunger cutter
embossing flower mat
vegetable oil and brush
2 1/2-in. circle cutter
pale green cupcake wrappers

Mix pink sugar paste by adding a small amount of red sugar paste to white sugar paste. Roll out the pink sugar paste to 1/4 in. thick and, using a craft knife, cut out a 1 1/4 x 3/4-in. rectangle. Smooth the top edge with your finger. Starting at one end, roll the sugar paste between your two fingers, pinching at the base, forming the rosebud. As you reach the end of the roll, pull the end over the bottom and pinch, to create the bud effect.

Roll out the green sugar paste to 1/4 in. thick and use the small leaf cutter to create the rose leaf. If you don't have a plunger cutter, which imprints the leaf veins, use a craft knife to make similar marks. Use a 2 1/2-in. circle cutter to cut the white sugar-paste round to place on the top of the cupcake. Spoon a tablespoon of buttercream onto the top of the cupcake. Place the embossed disc over the buttercream to cover the cupcake. Be careful not to smooth away the imprint. Create a small hole in the center of the cupcake and add the rosebud and rose leaf. Secure with edible glue, if needed. Repeat the process for each cupcake. Secure the cupcake wrappers around the liners to serve.

variations

primrose teapot cake

see base recipe page 183

primrose patterned teapot cake
Use a stencil and luster paint to decorate the teapot.

flowered teapot cake
Cut out sugar-paste flowers, paint them, and stick them on the teapot for a 3-D effect.

painted primrose cupcakes & cookies
Use the painting technique to paint flat-iced cupcakes or cookies.

teapot cupcake toppers
Cut out teapot shapes from sugar paste. Allow to dry. Paint with flowers and place on top of frosted cupcakes.

spotted teapot cake
Simplify by cutting out brightly colored sugar-paste circles to make a spotted teapot.

teapot party display
Serve painted, flat-iced cupcakes in teacups alongside the primrose teapot cake.

variations

rose posy cake

see base recipe page 185

miniature rose posy cupcakes
Create an individual rose using the same technique on a smaller scale to make a rose cupcake topper.

triple rose posy cake
Create three posies of roses and place on alternative sides of a multilayer cake.

rose posy handbag cake
Using the same technique, create a rose corsage for a large handbag cake.

rose posy waterfall cake
Use the roses as part of a mixed-flower waterfall effect down the front of a multilayer cake.

rose mini cake topper
Create a single rose in one shade of pink as a decoration for a mini cake.

variations

moth orchid cake

see base recipe page 186

moth orchid cupcakes
Create the orchid from sugar paste and place on top of a frosted cupcake.

moth orchid wedding cake
Create a three-layer cake, cover with white sugar paste, and arrange a spray of moth orchids.

purple moth orchid cake
Use edible luster dust and purple, brown, and yellow edible paint to make a purple moth orchid.

piped moth orchid cake
Use the orchid petal cutters to lightly indent a cake and use this as a guide to pipe the flowers with royal icing.

painted moth orchid cake
Mix food coloring with cocoa butter and paint moth orchids on the side of a cake.

variations

blossom cupcakes

see base recipe page 189

pearly blossom cupcakes
Add small pearl dragées to the center of each blossom before allowing them to dry.

shimmery blossom cupcakes
Spray the flowers with edible luster spray to give a glimmering effect.

blossom-covered mini cupcakes
Cover mini cupcakes with blossoms for a smaller bite.

heart-shaped blossom cupcakes
Flat-ice a cupcake with sugar paste and arrange the blossoms in a heart shape.

blossom cake
Use the blossoms to decorate a larger cake by laying a polka-dot pattern over the cake and using a pin to mark the pattern. Glue single blossoms on every pinprick to create a simple, beautiful design.

cherry blossom cupcake
Make the blossoms from pink sugar paste, and lay over light-green-frosted cupcakes.

tropical flowers cake

see base recipe page 190

tropical flower cupcakes
Sprinkle the crushed graham crackers over a frosted cupcake and decorate with a tropical flower.

blue tropical flower cake
Change the flower to blue by painting it with blue edible luster dust.

tropical beach cake
Mix blue and white sugar paste to create a sea effect when covering the cake.

lei cake
Create brightly colored flowers and place in a lei on top of a Hawaiian-inspired cake.

turqoise tropical flower cake
To create a turquoise flower, use green sugar paste and edible blue paint for the detail.

bougainvillea cake
Use four hot-pink sugar-paste petals per flower, and use a line tool to create a crinkle effect. Cover the sides of a white-iced cake with the flowers.

variations

summer vintage rose cupcakes

see base recipe page 192

summer vintage rose & bunting cupcakes
Create bunting from sugar-paste flags and attach to a flat-iced cupcake. Hand-paint roses on some of the flags.

rosebud cupcakes
Create same-color rosebuds out of sugar paste and position on a frosted cupcake.

stemmed rose cupcakes
Model a hot pink rose from sugar paste along with green leaves, and place on a frosted cupcake.

vintage polka-dot cupcakes
Lay sugar-paste dots on rolled-out sugar paste. Cover with plastic wrap and gently roll the dots flat. Cut circles to cover cupcakes.

simple strawberry cupcakes
Paint strawberries onto a flat-iced cupcake for a vintage summer feel.

variations

hand-piped rose cupcakes

see base recipe page 195

hand-piped rose cupcake bouquet
Create a mini cupcake bouquet: frost a mini cupcake with buttercream roses and affix to half a polystyrene ball in a flowerpot.

hand-piped rose centerpieces
Pipe individual roses onto greaseproof paper and place on cakes as centerpieces.

hand-piped rose swirl-covered cake
Change to a Wilton 1M or 2D tip. Start in the middle and, in one continuous movement, pipe around in a swirl to create the rose. Continue piping roses until the cake is covered.

hand-piped rose cupcake topper
Pipe onto a sugar-paste disc and place on an iced cupcake so that the rose sits at an angle.

hand-piped two-color rose cupcakes
Fill 2 piping bags with 2 tones of the same color. Start with the darkest and change bags for the lighter color after piping half a rose. This will create a pretty two-tone-effect rose.

shimmery hand-piped rose cupcakes
Sprinkle a little luster dust over the tips of the finished rose.

variations

vanity rose cake

see base recipe page 196

stripy vanity rose cake
Use royal icing to pipe lines up the side of the cake, finishing in the center of the cake top, then place the bloom on top.

vintage vanity rose cake
Add a vintage feel by adding lace ribbon to the cake.

quilted vanity rose cake
Use a quilting tool to add a quilting effect to your cake, then finish with the bloom.

vanity rose and pearl cake
Use royal icing and pipe pearls rising from the base of the cake, or create a polka-dot effect, and finish with the bloom.

vanity rose vine cake
Pipe green royal icing vines from the bloom and add sugar-paste leaves.

quilted flower cupcakes

see base recipe page 199

embossed cupcakes with rosebuds
Imprint the sugar paste with a flower embossing mat. Cut out a 2 1/2-in. circle and add to the top of a cupcake with 1 tablespoon of buttercream. Add a small rosebud and place on top of a frosted cupcake.

shimmery quilted flower cupcakes
Use gold, silver, or pearl edible luster spray to create a shimmery effect over the embossed or quilted sugar paste before adding the flower to the finished cupcake.

piped quilted flower cupcakes
Using royal icing and a PME no. 2 tip, pipe over the details of the embossed sugar-paste detail to create a 3-D effect.

quilted flower cupcakes with bows
Create a sugar-paste bow for the top of the quilted cupcake. Roll out a contrasting-color sugar paste and cut a 10 x 1 1/4-in. rectangle. Fold both ends into the center and pinch in place. Add a thin strip of sugar paste over the join. Place a small roll of paper towels between each loop to keep them in place while they dry. After an hour, glue onto the quilted cupcake with 2 sugar-paste bow tails.

variations

hydrangea cake & cupcake tower

see base recipe page 200

hydrangea cupcake tier
Arrange the hydrangea cupcakes on a tiered stand and alter the shade or colors of the hydrangeas on each stand.

hydrangea wedding cake
Make the hydrangea flowers from white sugar paste and cover the whole cake for a bridal feel. Perfect for a wedding.

midnight-colored hydrangea cake & cupcake tower
Cover the hydrangeas with edible silver luster, and use over a cake covered with dark-blue sugar paste, and cupcakes frosted with dark-blue frosting.

hydrangea cake pops
Use a single hydrangea flower to decorate cake pops as party favors or wedding favors.

summery hydrangea cake & cupcake tower
Use a mixture of pink, purple, and blue flowers for a more colorful summer feel.

variations

vintage rosebud cupcakes

see base recipe page 202

vintage rosebud and pearl-string cupcakes
To epitomize the vintage feel, add a ring of pearl dragées around the edge of the cupcake secured with edible glue, or pipe royal icing pearls around the edge using a Wilton no. 4 tip.

vintage rosebud embossed cupcakes
To create a different look, roll the white sugar paste with a flower embossing mat to create a 3-D raised pattern.

vintage valentine's cupcakes
Make 3 rosebuds in red sugar paste and place on top of a chocolate cupcake decorated with a chocolate buttercream swirl.

vintage rosebud bouquet cake
Use multiple rosebuds to circle the base of each layer of a multilayer cake. You can also cover the top layer surface with a bouquet of rosebuds. You can use a single color or a blend of the same color tones to create a more natural look.

piped vintage rosebud cupcakes
Instead of using sugar paste, pipe the rosebud using pink buttercream and a Wilton no. 104 tip. You can pipe directly onto a cupcake while continually turning to create a small bud. Or you can pipe the rosebud onto a flower nail; the bud can then be removed and placed onto a larger cake, if desired.

letters &
numbers

Take inspiration from the projects in this chapter

to make any message you want with sugar paste.

You might need to scale letters up or down to

make sure your message will fit on the cake as you

intend it to; it's a good idea to try it with paper

cutouts first.

lollipop name cake

see variations page 235

For very long names, make smaller lollipops to make sure they fit on the cake.

8-in. prepared cake covered with 50 percent
yellow and 50 percent white sugar paste mix
(pages 12, 20)
a selection of brightly colored sugar pastes,
including red, blue, green, yellow, and pink
brightly colored chocolate-covered candies

equipment
9-in. long lollipop sticks, 1 for each letter
medium alphabet cutters or letter tappits

Cover the cake with sugar paste on the same day that you make the lollipops (48 hours
before serving); the covering needs to be able to take the weight of the lollipops.

To create the lollipops, roll out 2 sausages of contrasting-color sugar paste, each 1/2 in. wide
and 4 in. long. Press the 2 sausages together and start to roll the center of the lollipop,
continually turning until complete. Trim the end and glue in place. Insert a large lollipop
stick from the end; join into the center of the lollipop. Repeat the process using different-
colored sugar paste for the amount of letters required. Roll out the red sugar paste to 1/10
in. thick and cut out the desired name letters. Glue onto the front of the lollipops. Allow to
dry for at least 48 hours.

Using a mixture of rolled and molded color sugar paste, create a selection of candy shapes to
decorate the side of the cake. Glue in place. Glue brightly colored chocolate-covered candies
around the base of the cake in an alternating pattern. Insert the lollipops at least halfway
into the cake and place brightly colored chocolate-covered candies around the base of the
lollipop sticks to hide the joins.

letter cupcakes

see variations page 236

Candy melts are available in many colors, but if you prefer, you could melt chocolate chips instead.

cupcakes baked in brown liners (page 16)
3 tbsp. buttercream per cupcake (page 19)
vegetable oil
candy melts

equipment
piping bag or Ziploc bag
letter molds

Prepare the letter molds by spraying them with a very small amount of vegetable oil, making sure you get right into the corners. Wipe off any excess with paper towels.

Melt the candy melts in a bowl over a saucepan of simmering water or in a microwave, then transfer to a piping bag or Ziploc bag with the corner snipped. Carefully pipe the candy melts into the molds. Gently tap the mold on a work surface to remove any bubbles.

Leave in a cool place to set. The refrigerator is fine for candy melts, but chocolate will develop a white bloom if placed in too cold a place. Cool room temperature is best. When set, gently remove the letters from the mold. Place letters on frosted cupcakes.

pirate cupcakes

see variations page 237

Ahoy, matey! For a pirate-themed celebration, make a flag with each guest's name on it and place on a cupcake as a party favor.

cupcakes baked in red polka-dot liners
  (page 16)
3 tbsp. buttercream per cupcake (page 19)

equipment
computer and color printer, paper, and scissors
paper glue
laminating machine and laminating pouches
  (optional)
scotch tape
lollipop or cake pop sticks

You can easily find free, printable cupcake-pick templates on the Internet or you can create and customize them yourself. For a child's face, print a picture of their face about 1 1/4 in. wide and cut it out. Download a pirate's cartoon hat and size to fit the child's head. Print, cut it out, and glue to the top of the head. You have the option to laminate the face at this stage, but it is not necessary. Laminating makes the picks food-safe (though obviously not edible!), and adds a professional finish. Use a piece of scotch tape to secure the lollipop stick to the back of the pick.

Other designs, including a skull and crossbones, can be downloaded and added to a circle template. This can be colored to match the pirate theme. You can also create a pirate's black flag with your child's name and birthday age in white text. To finish, simply frost the cupcakes and insert the picks into the top.

cake pop favors

see variations page 238

Get the birthday girl or boy to help with the dipping, swirling and number-punching.
Many hands make light work!

8 oz. store-bought pound cake
2 tbsp. buttercream (page 19)
12-oz. bag of Wilton yellow candy melts
pale blue sugar paste
multicolor small-circle sprinkles

equipment
3-tbsp. cookie scoop
cake pop sticks
small number cutters or tappits
polystyrene block
cellophane bags
ribbon

Remove the pound cake from the package and trim off the crust. Crumble the cake into a
bowl with your fingers until it resembles breadcrumbs. Add the buttercream and stir with
a fork until it combines. It should hold together but not be sticky. Using a 3-tablespoon
cookie scoop, form balls of the dough and roll in your hands. Place on a tray covered in
parchment paper and place in the refrigerator. Allow to set for at least 10 minutes.

Melt the candy melts in the microwave. Remove the cake balls from the refrigerator. Insert
the tops of the cake pop sticks into the candy melt, and then insert halfway into the cake
balls. Place back in the refrigerator. This allows the sticks to set.

Roll out the pale blue sugar paste to 1/10 in. thick and cut out your desired birthday number.
Remelt the candy melt in the microwave, if required. Remove the cake pops from the
refrigerator and dip into the candy melt, covering to the tip of the stick. To remove any
excess, twist over the bowl and gently tap the stick on the side until the dripping stops.

Before the cake pop sets, add the desired sugar-paste letter (check that it's the right way up for the favor) and sprinkle with the small-circle sprinkles.

Stand the cake pop to dry in a polystyrene block. Repeat the process for each cake pop. Once dry, place gently in a cellophane bag and secure with a ribbon.

initial rosette mini cake

see variations page 239

Replace the letter with a number 1, and change the colors to brighter shades to celebrate a team victory!

mini cake covered with white sugar paste
(pages 12, 20)
sugar paste in cream, light pink, green, and
dark pink

equipment
6 circle cutters varying in size
serif-font letter cutter or tappit

Roll out the cream, light pink, and green sugar paste to 1/10 in. thick in turn, and cut out 5 circles varying in size and color, keeping the smallest cutter to one side.

Start with the largest circle. Place the circle on your work mat and place a cocktail stick over the edge. Gently roll back and forth around the edge of the circle until you have created a ruffle effect. Repeat this process for all 5 circles. With the largest at the back and the smallest at the front, glue the ruffled circles together.

Using the smallest cutter, cut a cream circle. Roll out the dark pink sugar paste to 1/10 in. thick, using the letter cutter or tappit to cut out an initial. Affix it to the cream sugar-paste circle and glue in place on the rosette. Allow to dry overnight. When your rosette is dry, position in place on a mini cake.

golf cake

see variations page 240

Perfect for a retirement cake or a golf fan's birthday, this will be welcome at any clubhouse.

8-in. cake covered with pale green sugar paste
(pages 12, 20)
sugar paste in white, bottle green, light green,
brown, and gray
green buttercream

equipment
ball tool
small alphabet cutters or alphabet tappits
aluminum foil
white rectangle sticker or white paper and glue
piping bag
Wilton no. 233 grass tip

Create the golf balls by rolling white sugar paste and creating a 2-in. ball. Cut in half to create 2 semicircles. Repeat and make the desired number of golf balls. Using a small ball tool or skewer, imprint the golf balls with dimples.

Roll out the light green sugar paste to 1/8 in. and, using 2 1/4-in. alphabet cutters or tappits, cut out the desired letters and glue to the front of the golf balls. Allow to dry for 24 hours.

To make the golf bag, use bottle green sugar paste and mold into a kidney-shaped bag. Trim with white and green sugar paste, and insert a toothpick into the bottom halfway up.

To make the golf clubs, cover toothpicks with aluminum foil and top each with brown or gray sugar paste to look like different golf clubs. Imprint the tops with a craft knife. Insert clubs into the top of the golf bag and allow to dry for 24 hours.

Roll out the light green sugar paste and cut out a kidney-shaped green using a craft knife; it should be about half the size of the top of the cake. Glue onto the cake and create a golf hole using a skewer. Insert a toothpick covered in aluminum foil with a white sticker flag. Glue the golf balls on the front of the cake

Using a Wilton no. 233 grass tip, pipe green buttercream grass around the base of the cake and around the edge of the green. Insert the golf bag on top of the cake. Create a small white sugar-paste golf ball and glue onto the green.

bunting name cupcakes

see variations page 241

Rows of personalized pennants are very straightforward to make, and they look very impressive. A great project to use up scraps of sugar paste!

cupcakes baked in baby blue liners
   (page 16)
1 tbsp. buttercream per cupcake (page 19)
sugar paste in white and pale blue
blue gingham sugar sheet, 15 x 12 in.

equipment
2 1/2-in. round cutter
paper, pen, and scissors
small alphabet cutters or alphabet tappits

Roll out the white sugar paste to 1/4 in. thick and cut a 2 1/2-in. circle for each cupcake. Place 1 tablespoon of buttercream on the top of the baked cupcakes, then place the white sugar-paste disc on top, smoothing flat with your fingers.

Cut a flag template from paper to the size that fits your cupcake. Carefully remove the sugar sheet from the package. Place the template on the back of the sugar sheet and trace the number of flags required. Cut out the flags.

Roll out the pale blue sugar paste to 1/10 in. thick and cut out the letters required for your desired name. If you are using alphabet tappits, allow the sugar paste to crust for a few minutes before cutting out the letters, as this will help with their release.

Glue the letters onto the bunting flags and then glue the flags onto the tops of the cupcakes.

star name cake

see variations page 242

Create a cake featuring the name of your very own little star.

6-in. cake covered with pale blue sugar paste
  (pages 12, 20)
sugar paste in yellow, blue, green, red, and
  orange

equipment
2 1/2-in. star cookie cutter or template
silver floral wire (24-gauge)
medium alphabet cutters
1 1/4-in. star cutter

Roll out the yellow sugar paste to 1/2 in. thick and, using a 2 1/2-in. star cookie cutter or template, cut out the desired number of stars for your name. Dip 8-inch lengths of the floral wire into edible glue, insert into the bottom of the star, and push until halfway up. Lay flat and allow to dry for 24 hours.

Roll out the red sugar paste to 1/10 in. thick and use alphabet cutters to cut out the desired letters and glue to the front of the stars. From the same red sugar paste, cut three 1 1/4-in. stars. Also roll out 1/2-in. balls. You will need at least 2 balls of each color per wire. Repeat cutting out stars and rolling balls in the other sugar-paste colors. Now thread a red ball onto the wire and carefully push to the top until it reaches the star. Use edible glue to secure the ball in place. Repeat the process with the other colored balls in an alternating pattern. When you have at least 9 balls secured, repeat the process on the other stars. You should have at least 3 1/4 in. of wire remaining at the bottom.

Carefully insert the wires into the cake, spacing evenly across the top of the cake. Glue the 1 1/4-in. stars around the middle of the cake in alternating colors. Roll about 50 more 1/2-in. balls and glue around the base of the cake in an alternating pattern.

candy name cake

see variations page 243

When you need a last-minute cake, this will still impress! Pick the recipient's favorite candy for a personal touch.

rectangle cake covered with sugar paste
   (any color) (pages 12, 20)
selection of small candies, sprinkles, or
   nonpareils

equipment
paintbrush
brightly colored ribbon

Choose a cake that is long enough to fit the number of letters you require. Choose a selection of small candies and sprinkles that suit your name cake (e.g. boy, girl, adult). They should be smaller than 1/4-in. wide. Arrange the candies on the cake until you are happy with the design and know that the letters fit. Glue the candies in place with edible glue.

If you have chosen small sprinkles or nonpareils, first check that there is enough space in the design, then paint the desired letter on the cake in edible glue. Immediately sprinkle the nonpareils with your fingers until the letter is covered. Pat down to secure and use a dry paintbrush to remove any rogue sprinkles.

Place a coordinating brightly colored ribbon around the base of the cake and secure at the back with a pin.

shaped quinceañera rosette cake

see variations page 244

A Quinceañera is the traditional Latin American family celebration for girls on their fifteenth birthday. If you place your presentation board on a turntable, and secure with a little putty, you'll find it much easier to pipe the rosettes consistently.

12-in. round sponge cake (page 12)
21 3/4-in. square sponge cake (page 12)
18 oz. pink buttercream (page 19)
jam for filling

equipment
2-in. round cutter
piping bag
Wilton 1M tip
presentation cake board

Use a 2-in. round cutter to cut out the center of the round sponge cake. From the square cake, cut the number "1" shape by cutting a 10 x 3 1/4-in. rectangle. Cut the top of the number "5" and the adjacent vertical by cutting 2 rectangles, 12 x 2 1/2-in. each, from the same square cake. Cut the adjacent vertical top at a 45-degree angle to create the desired angle. Place next to the circle part of the number "5" and cut the gap from the ring. Trim the shape where needed. Use a remnant piece as the "flick" off the top of the number "1." Once you are happy with the shape of the numbers, you can cut the cake horizontally and sandwich with buttercream and jam. Join any of the parts together with the buttercream. Cover the entire cake with a thin layer of buttercream and place in the refrigerator to set for at least 1 hour.

Remove the cake from the refrigerator and place on the presentation cake board. Using a Wilton 1M tip, pipe 2-in.-wide roses on the sides of the cake. Start piping from the center and swirl in a circular motion outward. Continue to cover the top of the cake and create smaller swirled roses to fill in any gaps.

diamante craft letters cake

see variations page 245

Take great care to remove all of the diamante pieces, including the letter stickers, before serving, as they are not edible.

8-in. sponge cake covered with white sugar
    paste (pages 12, 20)

equipment
40-inch stitched-edge black grosgrain ribbon
diamante brooch
diamante acid-free craft stickers
diamante or metallic cake topper spray

Place the black ribbon around the base of the cake and secure at the back with a pin. Take 6 inches of the same ribbon and fold both ends into the center, overlapping slightly.

Take another piece a little more than 2 inches long and tie around the middle. Hold in place and affix to the front of the ribbon and cake with a single pin in the center of the bow.

Attach the diamante brooch by inserting its own pin into the center of the bow or by using a pin and fixing the brooch to the center of the bow.

Using edible glue, attach the diamante craft letters to the top of the cake. Prick a hole in the center of the cake and insert the cake topper spray.

variations

lollipop name cake

see base recipe page 215

lollipop name cupcakes

Use small round lollipops and add small sugar-paste numbers for the child's age. Insert into a cupcake baked in primary-color liners to look like balloons.

swirl-covered lollipop cake

Make a large cake shaped like a lollipop, covered in swirl sugar paste. Use the same technique as the lollipops by rolling 2 sausages of contrasting-color sugar paste into the swirl and placing on top of the cake. Add the child's name to the lollipop's stick.

swirl-covered lollipop cupcakes

Create lollipop cupcakes: spread 1 tablespoon of buttercream on top of a cupcake to act as glue. Use the same lollipop technique and create a contrasting-color sugar-paste swirl and place flat on top of the cupcake. Insert a lollipop into the front of the cupcake liner and add the child's age on the top of the cupcake, if desired.

bee mine cake

Instead of lollipops, make small bumblebees and place them on pop sticks; instead of the brightly colored candy around the base of the cake, place pink candy or sugar paste hearts; instead of the candy shapes on the sides of the cake, use 6–8 of the daises from page 55.

variations

letter cupcakes

see base recipe page 216

chocolate letter cake

Use chocolate letters to decorate a large cake.

hand-written chocolate letter cupcakes

Use melted chocolate in a Ziploc bag. Snip the corner and pipe letters onto greaseproof paper. Allow to set and place on top of cupcakes to spell out a name or greeting.

piped letter cupcakes

Flat-ice cupcakes with vanilla buttercream and pipe your message directly onto the cupcakes with chocolate buttercream.

multicolored letter cupcakes

Use candy melts to create different-colored alternate letters.

chocolate-dipped cookie letters

Cut cookies with letter cutters and dip in melted chocolate. Either serve as they are, or use as cupcake toppers.

variations

pirate cupcakes

see base recipe page 219

pirate message cupcakes
Create face picks with speech bubbles so your relatives can have their favorite sayings, or simply include "Happy Birthday" in the design of the cupcake picks.

bridal cupcake picks
Simple round cupcake picks incorporating the bride and groom's initials can be created to complement any wedding theme or color.

children's birthday picks
Include their favorite toys and characters, name, and birthday age.

flag cupcake picks
Flag-shaped cupcake picks are ideal for any occasion and can include any personal text desired. Ideal for charities and fundraisers.

edible cupcake toppers
Personalized edible icing toppers can easily be purchased on the Internet and can include names, pictures, logos, and even photos. These can then be transferred to sugar paste and added to the tops of cupcakes or cakes.

variations

cake pop favors

see base recipe page 220

wedding cake pop favors
Create cake pop favors in colors that match the wedding theme and add the bride's and groom's initials. Package and tie with a ribbon.

valentine cake pops
Create cake pops in pink covered with red heart sprinkles. Package in a cellophane bag and tie with a red ribbon. Add a "Be my Valentine?" label.

easter cake pops
Create cake pops by molding the dough into an egg shape and decorating with sprinkles. Package and tie with a spring ribbon.

halloween cake pops
Create cake pops in orange with sugar-paste "BOO" on the front and sprinkled with Halloween sprinkles such as black cats.

christmas cake pops
Create a selection of cake pops in green and red with sugar-paste "Ho" on the front and sprinkled with festive nonpareils.

variations

initial rosette mini cake

see base recipe page 223

button rosette mini cake
Replace the initial with a button for a vintage feel.

rosette wedding cake
Use a number of rosettes to decorate a multilayer wedding cake. On the top tier, place the bride's and groom's initials in the center of a large rosette.

mini rosette cupcake topper
Make a rosette from 3 circles and use to top a frosted cupcake.

theme-colored rosette mini cake
Adapt the colors to celebrate an occasion: red, white, and blue for the 4th of July, or dark green for St. Patrick's Day.

age rosette cake
Make the rosette big enough to sit on top of a large cake and place the recipient's age in the middle.

variations

golf cake

see base recipe page 224

golf cake with bunker
In addition to the green, create a bunker for the top of the cake. Crush 2 graham crackers in a bag to create fine sand. Paint the area on the cake with edible glue, sprinkle the sand, and pat down.

golf cupcakes
Use green sugar-paste flat icing, adding a hole and flagpole using the same techniques.

golf course cupcakes
Pipe green buttercream using a Wilton no. 233 grass tip, and add a chocolate foil-covered golf ball.

golf ball cupcakes
Using the same technique as for the golf ball, create a cupcake covered in white sugar paste and imprinted with a ball tool.

golf course cupcakes cake
Place the desired number of cupcakes close together on a cake board. Use green buttercream to frost the grass with a Wilton no. 233 grass tip. Add graham-cracker crumb bunkers and a green sugar-paste green. You can also decorate with a sugar-paste river, trees, rocks, flowers, and a model golfer.

variations

bunting name cupcakes

see base recipe page 227

bright bunting cupcakes
Use primary-color sugar paste to create a carnival, festival, or child's birthday bunting.

happy birthday bunting cupcakes
Use alphabet cutters or tappits to spell "Happy Birthday" with a letter on each cupcake.

painted bunting cupcakes
Hand-paint the bunting with flowers and add dark-color sugar-paste letters such as hot pink. Ideal for a woman's birthday.

christmas bunting cupcakes
Create Christmas stocking bunting in red and green sugar paste with white tops. You could pipe or use an edible pen to write your relatives' names on each stocking.

variations

star name cake

see base recipe page 228

heart name cake
Change the stars to pink hearts using a 2 1/2-in. heart cookie cutter. You could use a mix of red and pink shades in the surrounding hearts and balls.

painted star name cake
Instead of using alphabet cutters and sugar paste to make the letters, use edible paint or edible pens to write the letters.

stacked star name cake
Instead of using balls on the wires, use cubes and stack them at adjacent angles. Roll out the sugar paste to 1/2 in. thick and then cut 1/2-in.-wide strips, from which you can cut 1/2-in. cubes.

star name cupcake toppers
Create coordinating cupcake star toppers by rolling out the sugar paste to 1/4 in. thick and cutting 1 1/4-in.-wide stars in a selection of matching colors.

star name cake with cake pops
Instead of using wires, use the cake pop technique: cut 2 1/2-in. stars from the dough, cover in yellow candy melts, and add the sugar-paste letters. Simply insert into the top of the cake in the same fashion.

candy name cake

see base recipe page 231

candy name cupcakes
To complement the cake, you could flat-ice cupcakes with the matching sugar paste, and arrange the same candies and sprinkles in the shape of the number age of the birthday.

candy name cake with candy stick border
Use multicolor candy sticks to make a border around the sides of the cake. These can be glued in place with edible glue.

monochrome candy name cake
Instead of using lots of colors of candy, pick out all-blue or all-red, etc.

love heart valentine's cake
Create a personalized Valentine's cake by using love heart candies to spell your desired name.

candy christmas cake
Create a "Happy Holidays" or "Ho Ho Ho!" Christmas message cake using a selection of festive candies and sprinkles. Place mini candy canes around the side of the cake.

chocolate chip name cake
Use a double-wide layer of chocolate chips to pick out the name over a contrasting-colored buttercream-frosted cake.

variations

shaped quinceañera rosette cake

see base recipe page 233

shaped quinceañera polka-dot cake
Use the same technique to carve the number cakes, but after the cake has set in the refrigerator, cover with sugar paste rolled out to 1/4 in. thick. Smooth over the edges with your hands and smooth the top with a cake smoother. Trim any excess. Glue on small sugar paste spots, and smooth over.

age number cake
Use the same technique to carve the number to create "18," "21," or any other special birthday age.

bridal shower initial cake
Use the same technique to carve an initials cake for a bride and groom. Ideal for a bridal shower.

rosette cupcakes
Use the same swirl rose piping technique to cover the top of complementing cupcakes.

shaped name rosette cake
Use the same technique to carve smaller letters. Ideal for a child's name birthday cake or christening cake.

diamante craft letters cake

see base recipe page 234

diamante initial cake
Use store-bought diamante cake topper initials for an effective and sparkly wedding cake topper (e.g. "W & M").

diamante age topper cake
Use store-bought diamante cake toppers for a required age.

diamante trimmed cake
Use a diamante trim around the base of the cake and ribbon.

diamante jewelry tier cake
Use diamante flower cake jewelry to flow down the front of a multilayer cake.

quilted diamante cake
Create a padded effect on a larger cake by scoring the quilt with a blade tool and studding the joins with diamante pins.

quilted diamante cupcakes
Cut 3 1/2 in circles of white sugar paste, scoring a quilt pattern with a blade tool and studding the joins with diamante pins. Place on top of flat-iced cupcakes.

animals

Totally adorable animal cakes and cupcakes are fun
to make and fun to present. Take a walk on the wild
side with a jungle-themed cupcake spread, or let
your imagination run free to make alien- and
dinosaur-decorated treats.

dinosaur cake

see variations page 270

No-one knows what color dinosaurs were, so you can make it in green, brown, or purple with yellow spots!

cake covered with green sugar paste
  (pages 12, 20)
sugar paste in green, black, white,
  and yellow

equipment
paper, pen, and scissors
cobblestone impression mat
blade tool
selection of small circle cutters

Start by making a paper template of your dinosaur. You want to fill as much of the cake as possible. Roll out the green sugar paste and place your template on top; use a craft knife to cut around your template. You don't need to cut the head out at this time. The size of your impression mat will dictate how many pieces you will need to make your dinosaur. Cut your dinosaur body into sections big enough for your impression mat to cover. Place the mat over each section and press down either with the palm of your hand or a rolling pin. Once each section has been textured, arrange the body back together on the cake and glue in place. Use a blade tool to define the legs.

Cut out the head shape. Use some green sugar paste rolled into a ball and flattened with your finger to make the nose. Use the skewer to add nostrils, and indent a mouth with a craft knife. Use the black and white sugar paste to mold the eyes. Cut two green semicircles and glue to the eyes to form the eyelids. Glue the nose and eyes to the face and position on the cake. Use some white sugar paste to add toes. Roll out and cut a selection of yellow sugar paste circles with circle cutters, and glue them along the back and tail.

monkey cupcakes

see variations page 271

These make great cupcake toppers, or you could use a selection of monkey, lion, tiger, zebra, and rhino toppers (page 271), and use to decorate a large cake in a jungle theme.

cupcakes baked in brown liners (page 16)
3 tbsp. buttercream per cupcake (page 19)
sugar paste in dark brown, light brown, pink,
   and black

equipment
2-in. round cutter
1 1/4-in.-wide heart cutter
piping tip (small size)

Roll the dark brown sugar paste to 1/4 in. thick and cut out the monkey's face using the 2-in. round cutter. Roll out the light brown sugar paste to 1/10 in. thick, and use a 1 1/4-in.-wide heart-shaped cutter to create the eyebrows. Glue to the monkey's face.

Roll a 3/4-in. ball out of light brown sugar paste. Press the ball flat to create the monkey's snout, about 2 1/4 in. wide. Glue to the center of the monkey's face. Imprint the mouth with the end of a piping tip to create the cheeky smile.

To create the ears, roll out two small 1/4-in. balls of light brown sugar paste and press flat with your finger. Add a smaller ball of pink sugar paste and press to create the inner ear. Pinch one end of the circle to create the ear shape and glue to the side of the head. Add small black sugar-paste eyes and a nose. Repeat the process for each cupcake. Allow to dry for 24 hours, then place on top of frosted cupcakes.

pig cupcakes

see variations page 272

Make a whole farmyard set of cupcakes with the variations on page 272.

cupcakes baked in pink liners (page 16)
3 tbsp. buttercream per cake (page 19)
sugar paste in pale pink and black

equipment
2-in. round cutter
Wilton 1M tip
piping bag

Roll out the pink sugar paste to 1/4 in. thick. Cut out a 2-in. circle with the round cutter for the face. Roll a 3/4-in. ball out of pink sugar paste. Press the ball flat, about 1 1/4 in. wide, to create the snout. Use a skewer to mark the nose and a metal piping tip to imprint the mouth. To create the ears, roll out 2 small 1/4-in. balls of pink sugar paste and press flat with your finger. Pinch each end of the circle to create the ear shape.

Glue the parts together, and add 2 small black fondant balls for the eyes and thinly rolled pink fondant for the hair. Repeat the process for each cupcake. Allow to dry for at least 24 hours. Pipe the buttercream onto the cupcakes in a swirl pattern and create a peak. Place the pigs on top of the frosted cupcakes.

teddy bear cake

see variations page 273

For a shaggier fur effect, you could use a Wilton's no. 233 grass tip to pipe coffee buttercream all over the body, arms, legs, and face of this sweet little bear.

6-in. cake covered in white sugar paste
   (pages 12, 20)
sugar paste in light brown, white, black, and
   light pink

equipment
ball tool

Roll a 2-in. ball out of light brown sugar paste for the body and shape into a teardrop. Roll a 1 1/4-in. ball out of light brown sugar paste for the head and flatten slightly with your finger.

Use some white sugar paste to lighten some chocolate sugar paste, creating light brown. Mold a snout and affix to the head. Indent a mouth and create a nose out of chocolate sugar paste. Roll 2 small black sugar-paste eyes. Roll 2 ears from the light brown sugar paste, flatten them, and indent the center with the ball tool and pinch to a point to create each ear.

Make 2 holes in the head and glue the points of each ear in the holes. Roll out sausage shapes for the arms and legs, and glue in place. Insert a cocktail stick into the neck of the teddy bear, leaving enough protruding to hold the head. Affix the head in place. Using a craft knife, texture the teddy bear's fur with small cuts. Add a baby pink sugar-paste bow to the head. Allow to dry for 48 hours. Place teddy bear on top of the frosted cake.

teddy bear-shaped cake

see variations page 274

Before piping the fur, make sure the cake is sat on a board with a large lip or handle at the back, to enable an easy transfer to the refrigerator without disturbing the frosting.

five 6-in. round sponge cakes (page 12)
chocolate buttercream (page 19)
sugar paste in light brown and black

equipment
serrated kitchen knife
2 1/2-in. round cutter
4 3/4-in. round cutter
piping bag
star tip

Layer three of the 6-inch sponge cakes on top of each other, sandwiching with buttercream between. Slice off the back 2 in. of the cake (keep the remnants for later). Trim the top cake with curved edges to create the shoulders. Using a 2 1/2-in. round cutter, cut 3 circles from one of the other sponge cakes to create the ears and snout. Take the final round cake and trim to create a 4-in. circular face. Attach the ears with buttercream and secure with a toothpick. Insert a skewer into the body of the cake, ensuring at least 4 in. are sticking out. Insert the head onto the skewer, at a slight angle. Using some of the cake remnants, add arms to the side of the body with buttercream and secure with a toothpick. Using more cake remnants, create legs and paws. Secure with buttercream and toothpicks.

Roll out the light brown sugar paste to 1/4 in. thick and cut out a 4 3/4-in. circle. Mold around the snout and smooth. Place the chocolate buttercream into a piping bag with a star tip, and pipe the fur all over the teddy bear. Add light brown sugar-paste paws and ears. Add a black sugar-paste nose, eyes, and smiley mouth. Allow to sit overnight in the refrigerator. Remember to remove the toothpicks and skewers before serving.

ladybug mini cupcakes

see variations page 275

These little bug cakes are super cute, super tasty, and super easy to make.

mini cupcakes baked in brown liners (page 16)
1 tbsp. chocolate buttercream per mini cupcake
    (page 19)
red chocolate-covered candies, such as M&M's
green sugar paste
crumbs of half a mini Oreo cookie (or
    equivalent) per mini cupcake

equipment
black edible pen
large leaf cutter
vein or blade tool

Using the black edible pen, carefully draw a smiley mouth on a red candy and draw two black dots for eyes. Then draw the rest of the ladybug's back with black spots. Allow to dry for a few minutes.

Meanwhile, roll out the green sugar paste to 1/10 in. thick, and either use a large leaf cutter or cut a large leaf shape by freehand with a craft knife. Using a vein or blade tool, mark the veins of the leaf. Attach the ladybug to the center of the green leaf with a dot of edible glue.

Repeat the process for each cupcake. Allow to dry for 24 hours. Frost the cupcakes with chocolate buttercream and immediately dip into the Oreo crumbs to create a soil effect. Place ladybugs on top of frosted cupcakes.

poodle cupcakes

see variations page 276

The hardest part of these poodles is the piping of the ears; practice on a board until you can pipe long strands of evenly thick lines. You can scoop your practice pipes back into the bag.

cupcakes baked in pink cupcake liners (page
    16)
3 tbsp. pink buttercream per cupcake (page 19)
sugar paste in light pink, dark pink, and black
marshmallows

equipment
piping bag
Wilton no. 233 tip
Wilton no. 4 tip

Using the light pink sugar paste, mold a snout for the poodle. Using the black sugar paste, make the nose and eyes. Glue the nose to the snout and add a darker pink tongue.

Take a marshmallow and cut in half horizontally. Place the smaller taper on the cupcake to act as the neck. Sit the other half on top at a 90-degree angle with the cut side of the marshmallow facing the front; stick the snout onto this side.

Place the pink buttercream in a piping bag with a no. 233 grass tip, and pipe short fur all over the marshmallow. Place the eyes in position.

In one motion, pipe each ear: start at the top and, using even pressure, bring the icing down and back up to the starting point to create a loop. Change the piping tip to a no. 4 and pipe curls on top of the poodle's head. Finish by placing a dark pink sugar-paste bow on the poodle's head. Repeat the process for each cupcake.

tabby cat cupcakes

see variations page 277

If you're making a lot of these tabby cat faces, roll a larger amount of the gray sugar paste into a tube, remove a "V"-shaped wedge from along the long side, and fill in with white sugar paste. Wrap, chill, and cut into slices. Roll each slice flat, and cut out with the circle cutter.

cupcakes baked in hot pink liners (page 16)
1 tbsp. buttercream per cupcake (page 19)
sugar paste in gray, white, black, and pink

equipment
plastic wrap
2 1/2-in. circle cutter

Roll out a small amount of both the gray and white sugar paste to 1/4 in. thick. Cut and remove a "V" shape in the gray sugar paste. Cut a "V" shape from white sugar paste. Lightly glue and push together. Cover with plastic wrap and gently roll over with the rolling pin. Unwrap, and use the circle cutter to cut a circle the same size as your cupcake so that the "V" shape is center, and affix to the cupcake with the buttercream.

Use the black sugar paste to cut stripes, whiskers, eyes, and a mouth, and glue in place. Using gray sugar paste, mold an ear. Cut a piece of pink sugar paste for the inner ear and press together. Repeat for the other ear and glue in place. Using the pink sugar paste, mold a nose and tongue, and glue in place. Repeat the process for each cupcake. Allow to dry for 24 hours before placing on flat-frosted cupcakes.

under-the-sea cake with fish cake pops

see variations page 278

Having a pool party? This is the cake for you. See page 278 for the starfish, crab, shark, and octopus pops.

store-bought pound cake, crumbled
2 tsp. buttercream per cake pop (page 16)
Wilton green candy melts
8-in. cake covered in blue-and-white marbled
    sugar paste (pages 12, 20)
sugar paste in purple, white, green, pink, yellow,
    and peach

equipment
3-tbsp. cookie scoop
5 cake pop sticks
polystyrene block
black edible pen

To create the fish cake pops, remove the pound cake from the package and trim the crust off the cake. Add the buttercream and stir with a fork until it combines. It should hold together but not be sticky. With the cookie scoop, form balls of the dough and roll in your hands. Place on a baking sheet covered in parchment paper and put in the refrigerator. Allow to set for at least 10 minutes. Melt the candy melts in the microwave. Remove the cake balls from the refrigerator. Insert the tops of the cake pop sticks into the candy melt, and then insert halfway into the cake balls. Place back in the refrigerator. Allow the sticks to set.

Roll out the purple sugar paste to 1/4 in. thick and cut out the fins and tail for the fish. Indent with a craft knife. Remelt the candy melt in the microwave, if required. Remove the cake pops from the refrigerator and dip into the candy melt, covering to the tip of the stick. To remove any excess, twist over the bowl until the dripping stops. Before the cake pops set, add fish fins and tails, and round white eyes. Dot the eyes with a black edible pen. Stand the cake pops to dry in a polystyrene block. Once dry, insert into the cake. Decorate the sides of the cake with sugar-paste seaweed, coral, and shells.

monster mini cake

see variations page 279

For a child's birthday celebration, or for Halloween, this set of not-so-scary monsters are as much fun to make as they are to eat! The instructions here are for the pink monster; see page 279 for the instructions for the blue and purple monsters too.

mini cakes (page 12)
6 tbsp. buttercream per cake, mixed with food
    paste coloring of your choice (page 19)
sugar paste in red, white, and black

equipment
 lollipop stick
piping bag
Wilton no. 104 grass tip

Roll a 2 1/4-in. ball of white sugar paste for an eyeball. Mix a small amount of red sugar paste with some white to create pink for the eyelid. Roll out the pink sugar paste and cut out a 2 1/4-in. circle; affix to the eyeball with edible glue or water. Add a small black sugar-paste eye pupil. Add a lollipop stick into the base of the eyeball and allow to dry for 24 hours.

To create the monster's mouth, roll out black sugar paste to 1/10 in. thick and cut out a large smiley mouth. Add sharp white teeth and a pink tongue.

Ice the mini cake with buttercream and place in the refrigerator for at least 1 hour. Place the colored buttercream in a piping bag with a Wilton no. 104 grass tip. Place the cake on a plate or cake turntable, and start piping the hair from the bottom. Pipe in circles until you have totally covered the cake. While the buttercream is still wet, add the mouth and insert the eyeball into the top of the cake.

alien cupcakes

see variations page 280

A close encounter of the cupcake kind.

cupcakes baked in lime green liners (page 16)
1 tbsp. buttercream per cupcake (page 19)
2 marshmallows per cupcake
sugar paste in green, acid yellow, white, and
    black
red licorice laces

equipment
3-in. round cutter
large cupcake pods (2 1/2-in. base)

Cut one of the marshmallows horizontally and attach its sticky side to the top of the other half to create the body of the alien. Attach the marshmallow body to the top of the cupcake with a tablespoon of buttercream.

Mix lime green sugar paste by adding a small amount of green sugar paste to the acid yellow. Roll out the lime green sugar paste to 1/4 in. thick and cut a large circle using the 3-in. round cutter. Place the lime green circle over the marshmallow body and arrange the skirts evenly.

To create the alien's eye, roll a small ball of white sugar paste and flatten with your finger. Add a black sugar-paste pupil. Repeat for each alien and glue to the front of the body. Using a skewer, create a hole on each side of the alien's head. Insert 1 3/4-in. pieces of red licorice laces into each of the holes to create the alien's antennae. Repeat for each alien.

Place each cupcake into a clear plastic cupcake pod, to look like it is traveling in a spaceship.

butterfly cake & cupcake tower

see variations page 281

Such a simple, pretty design; you'll find yourself making it time and time again!

prepared cake covered with white sugar paste,
    with a pink satin ribbon around the base
cupcakes baked in silver liners (page 16)
3 tbsp. buttercream per cupcake (page 19)
sugar paste in pink and white

equipment
cardboard and scissors
2-in. wide butterfly cutter
1 1/4-in. wide butterfly cutter
silver floral wire (24-gauge)

Create a butterfly drying rack by cutting a piece of 4-inch-wide cardboard and folding it in half, supported at 90 degrees. This allows the butterflies to dry in position. Roll the pink sugar paste to 1/4 in. thick and cut out the butterfly shape using the 2-in. butterfly cutter. Roll a small sausage shape out of white sugar paste to create the body and glue in place. Mark the wings with a craft knife or blade tool. Repeat the process to create white butterflies with pink bodies. Place in drying rack and allow to dry for 24 hours.

To create the butterfly cake topper spray, repeat the process of making the butterflies, but use the smaller butterfly cutter. Before drying, place 6 inches of floral wire into edible glue and insert halfway up the center of the butterfly. Repeat at least 12 times in the 2 colors, as they are delicate and this allows for breakage. Place on the drying rack for 24 hours.

When dry, gently insert the butterflies on wires into the top of the cake at least 2 in. deep. Arrange the wires to create an even spray. Place a 2-in. butterfly on top of each frosted cupcake, perched at an angle to look like resting butterflies.

variations

dinosaur cake

see base recipe page 247

dinosaur cupcake topper
Create a dinosaur cutout for cupcakes, using the texture mat for the whole area.

carved dinosaur
Make a 3-D cake shaped like a dinosaur and cover with the textured sugar paste.

alien cake
Use the same effect to create an alien cake or a monster cake.

piped dinosaur cake
Use the same template for the dinosaur and texture by piping on green buttercream through a star tip.

fire-breathing dragon cake
Adapt the technique to create a fire-breathing dragon, using red and yellow sugar-paste circles for the fire. Great for a knight and princess party.

monkey cupcakes

see base recipe page 248

tiger cupcakes

Cut a 2-in. round face from orange sugar paste and add an orange sugar-paste snout. Indent the mouth and prick the snout with a toothpick. Create the ears using the same technique as the monkey, but using orange and pink sugar paste. Roll black sugar paste to 1/10 in. thick and cut tiger stripes; add to the face and snout.

lion cupcakes

Create a pale yellow sugar paste and cut the head using a 2-in. round cutter. Roll 1/4-in. balls, press flat, and pinch to create hair; repeat around the head to create a mane. Add a pale yellow face and ears made like the tiger. Add eyes, nose, and mouth, and prick the snout with a toothpick.

rhino cupcakes

Create pale blue-gray sugar paste. Roll out and cut out a 2-in. round face. Add snout, ears, and eyes, and mark the mouth and snout with a toothpick. Mold horns out of white sugar paste and add above the snout.

zebra cupcakes

Cut a 2-in. round face out of white sugar paste. Add a light brown sugar-paste snout, and make the ears like the tiger using white and light brown sugar paste. Cut thin strips of black fondant like the tiger's stripes, and add to the face. Add eyes and mark the mouth and snout with a toothpick.

variations

pig cupcakes

see base recipe page 251

duck cupcakes
Roll out the yellow sugar paste and cut a 2-in. circle. Cut a beak shape from rolled orange sugar paste and glue to the center of the face. Add black eyes and a tuft of yellow hair. Place on top of frosted cupcakes baked in yellow liners.

horse cupcakes
Create the face, snout, and ears like the pig, but out of brown sugar paste. Add white face markings and a light brown mane. Glue together and add black eyes. Place on top of frosted cupcakes baked in brown liners.

sheep cupcakes
Create the face using white sugar paste and a 2-in. scalloped-edge round cutter. Use a 1/2-in. flower plunger cutter to create the snout and imprint the nose with a toothpick. Create a tuft of hair with the same flower plunger cutter. Glue together with ears and black eyes. Place on top of frosted cupcakes baked in white liners.

cow cupcakes
Create the face out of white sugar paste using a 2-in. round cutter. Create black face markings using a scalloped-edge round cutter. The black tuft of hair can be made using a flower plunger cutter. Create ears and a snout like the pig and glue together with black eyes. Create a small yellow flower with a 1/4-in. flower cutter and glue to the mouth. Place on top of frosted cupcakes baked in black liners.

teddy bear cake

see base recipe page 252

teddy bear cupcakes
Make smaller, less detailed teddy bears for cupcakes, which could be created in various colors to suit boys or girls.

bear cupcake cake
Arrange cupcakes in a bear shape and pipe with a star tip using chocolate buttercream. Add sugar-paste eyes, nose, and ears.

panda bear cake
Create a panda bear in black and white sugar paste. Change the shape of the head and add black patches around the eyes.

koala bear cake
Make a koala bear in gray sugar paste with a white tummy and large black nose.

polar bear cake
Create a polar bear from white sugar paste. Elongate the snout and add a black nose. Perfect for Christmas cakes.

variations

teddy bear-shaped cake

see base recipe page 255

shaggy fur cake
Use a Wilton no. 233 grass tip to create a different "shaggy" fur effect.

girl teddy bear cake
Create a girl teddy bear by using pink buttercream and adding a hot pink sugar-paste bow next to one of its ears.

teddy bear with number cake
Make a sugar-paste number to represent the birthday age and place so the bear is holding the number.

reclining teddy bear cake
Create a teddy bear cake that is lying flat. Use the same technique to carve the body parts, but there is no need to use the toothpicks or skewers to secure the construction.

teddy bear face cake
Use cupcake sponges as the ears and snout. Use the same piping technique to decorate the face.

ladybug mini cupcakes

see base recipe page 256

bumblebee mini cupcakes
Use a black edible pen on a yellow candy to create a smiley face and black lines across its back. Roll out some white sugar paste and cut a small heart shape or use a 1/2-in-wide heart cutter. Fold the heart in half and glue to the back of the bumblebee. Attach to a green sugar-paste leaf.

caterpillar mini cupcakes
Use a black edible pen to draw a smiley face on a blue hard candy. Using blue sugar paste, roll a ball 3/4 in. wide and another ball 1/2 in. wide. Glue the face onto a green sugar-paste leaf, then another blue candy, and then the sugar-paste balls as the tail.

snail mini cupcakes
Roll green sugar paste into a long sausage shape, 2 1/2 in. long and 1/4 in. wide. Start from one end and twist the sugar paste to form a snail shell. Press gently to secure the shape. Glue to a yellow sugar-paste body and, when dry, add a smiley face with a black edible pen.

dragonfly mini cupcakes
Roll some sugared licorice flat and, with scissors, cut out 2 dragonfly wings. Use a black edible pen to create a smiley face on an orange candy and glue to an orange sugar-paste body. Attach the wings to the back with edible glue and place on a green sugar-paste leaf.

variations

poodle cupcakes

see base recipe page 259

shih tzu cupcakes
Fill half the piping bag with chocolate buttercream and half with vanilla buttercream, and pipe over marshmallows.

scottie dog cupcakes
Mold dog from black or white sugar paste. Create fur texture using a craft knife. Add sugar-paste features.

labrador cupcakes
Mold dog from black or brown sugar paste. Add features and paint nose with confectioners' glaze for a wet effect.

dog silhouette cupcakes
Cut a dog silhouette from rolled-out sugar paste and use to decorate cupcakes or larger cakes, or to embellish handbag cakes.

dog face cupcakes
Use a star tip to pipe a dog's furry face straight onto a cupcake and add sugar-paste eyes, nose, and mouth.

variations

tabby cat cupcakes

see base recipe page 260

ginger tomcat cupcakes
Use orange, brown, and tan sugar paste to create a ginger tomcat.

girl tabby cat cupcakes
Use a mixture of pink tones to create a girly cat. Add a bow or hearts to her ear.

tiger cupcakes
Use orange, black, and white sugar paste to create a tiger. Add some teeth to the mouth.

cheetah cupcakes
Use tan sugar paste and add black spots to make a cheetah. Use a black edible pen to make the tear-shape eyes.

tabby cat cake
Adopt the same technique to cover and decorate a large cake.

variations

under-the-sea cake with fish cake pops

see base recipe page 263

crab cake pops
Using orange sugar paste, mold 2 legs with claws and 2 additional legs, each 1 1/4 in. long. Use the same technique to create the cake pops, and while the candy melt is still wet, add the claws and legs. Add white eyes, dotted with a black edible pen, and a smiley mouth.

octopus cake pops
Use the same technique to create the cake pops, and while the candy melt is still wet, add red licorice laces as legs. Add white eyes, dotted with a black edible pen, and a smiley mouth.

shark cake pops
Using sugar paste, create a dorsal fin, tail fin, and a mouth with sharp teeth. Use the same technique to create the cake pops, and while the candy melt is still wet, add the fins and mouth. Add white eyes, dotted with a black edible pen.

starfish cake pops
Use the same technique to create the cake pop, but shape the dough into a star instead of a ball. While the candy melt is still wet, add sugar disc sprinkles for the spots. Add white eyes, dotted with a black edible pen, and a smiley mouth.

monster mini cake

see base recipe page 264

one-eyed monster mini cake

Mold a white sugar-paste eyeball and cut in half. Add a black sugar-paste pupil and yellow eyelid. Allow to dry. Color the buttercream with yellow and blue food paste and place in separate piping bags with star tips. Start from the bottom and pipe the fur, pulling away upward. Alternate the colors. Add the eye to the front and lemon lollipops to the top as antennae.

furry purple monster mini cake

Mold two 1 1/4-in. balls of white sugar paste and add 2 black sugar-paste pupils. Color the buttercream with grape food paste and use a round tip to pipe the fur on the prepared mini cake. Start from the base and work up. Add the googly eyes to the top of the cake.

large monster cake

Create 6 cake-pop googly eyes and add to the top of a large cake decorated with colored buttercream piped with a star tip. Add a sugar-paste mouth and teeth.

halloween horned monster cake

Cover a large cake with red sugar paste. Mold googly eyes and a mouth with Dracula-style teeth that can be glued to the front of the cake. Mold 2 black sugar-paste horns and add to the top of the cake.

variations

alien cupcakes

see base recipe page 267

halloween ghost cupcakes

Bake cupcakes in white liners and use white sugar paste. Add eyes and a circle mouth with a black edible pen.

spider cupcakes

Bake cupcakes in black liners and attach 8 black licorice-lace legs into the buttercream before placing the black sugar-paste body on top. Add white sugar-paste eyes and use a black edible pen to add pupils to the eyes.

jellyfish cupcakes

Bake cupcakes in pink liners and use pink sugar paste. Cut pastel-colored rice paper into strips and fold into concertina shapes. Attach to the buttercream on top of the cupcakes and then add the jellyfish body on top. Add eyes and a smiley mouth with a black edible pen.

crab cupcakes

Bake cupcakes in red liners and attach 4 red licorice-lace legs into the buttercream before placing the red sugar paste body on top. Mold 2 red sugar-paste claws and attach to the side of the body. Add white sugar-paste eyes to the top and use a black edible pen to add black pupils and a smiley mouth.

variations

butterfly cake & cupcake tower

see base recipe page 268

spotted butterfly cake & cupcake tower
Add alternating colored spots on the butterfly wings.

painted butterfly cake & cupcake tower
Use a selection of edible pens or paints to create an Admiral butterfly.

sparkly butterfly cake & cupcake tower
Use colored luster dust to highlight edges of a plain-colored sugar-paste butterfly.

pearly butterfly cupcake topper
Cut a butterfly from sugar paste and glue to a flat-iced cupcake. Decorate the wings with edible pearl sprinkles.

butterfly cookie favors
Create butterfly cookie favors for a wedding. Cover butterfly-shape shortbread cookies with sugar paste, cut using the same cookie cutter. Decorate with a selection of sprinkles to match the wedding theme.

index